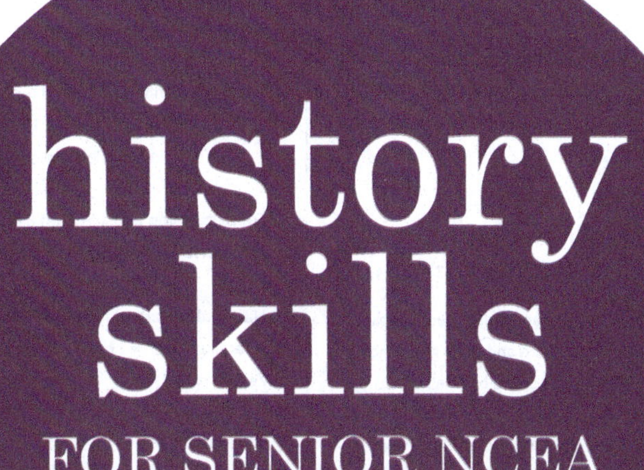

history skills

FOR SENIOR NCEA

The past is another country: skills for helping you navigate it

GRAEME BALL

NELSON
A Cengage Company

Australia • Brazil • Mexico • Singapore • United Kingdom • United States

History Skills for Senior NCEA
1st Edition
Graeme Ball

Cover designer: Cheryl Smith, Macarn Design
Text designer: Cheryl Smith, Macarn Design
Production controller: Siew Han Ong

Acknowledgements
Shutterstock: Front cover and pages 4, 7, 18, 22 *(right)*, 24, 37, 41, 63, 98, 104, 107.

Alexander Turnbull Library: Page 8, Group portrait of an unidentified Wanganui family with their possessions. Shows the mother, father, and small girl standing and seated beside a table with a sewing machine and caged bird on it. The man is also resting a Collins "Globe Dictionary of the English Language" on his knee. Photograph taken by William James Harding. Ref: 1/4-007838-F. Page 13, National Council of Women, Christchurch, 1896. Ref: 1/2-041798-F. Page 26, 1879 By: Walsh, Philip, 1843-1914, Ref: 1/4-012533-F. Page 28, Reconstruction of the signing of the Treaty of Waitangi by King, Marcus, 1891-1983 Ref: NON-ATL-0173. Page 84, Shows women harvesting what is probably kumara. Photograph taken circa 1910s by the Northwood brothers. Ref: 1/1-006265-G.

Public domain: Page 22, *(left)* Canadian machine gunners dig themselves into shell holes on Vimy Ridge. This shows squads of machine gunners operating from shell-craters in support of the infantry on the plateau above the ridge. Canadian Archives. Page 38, Parade of SA troops past Hitler, Nuremberg 1935. Page 40, Women cheer in front of Trinity College, Dublin as United States President Barack Obama and First Lady Michelle Obama are introduced to a large crowd before an address by the President at College Green in Dublin, Ireland, 23 May 2011. US Federal Government. Page 45, Jan. 20, 2009 'President-elect Barack Obama was about to walk out to take the oath of office. Backstage at the U.S. Capitol, he took one last look at his appearance in the mirror.' (Official White House photo by Pete Souza). US Federal Government. Page 58, 'At the bus station in Durham, North Carolina.' May 1940, Jack Delano. US Federal Government. Page 62, 'The Huns at the Battle of Chalons' from page 135 of *A Popular History of France From The Earliest Times* Volume I of VI. Illustration by A. De Neuville (1836-1885). Page 72, The Waitangi Sheet of the Treaty of Waitangi, signed between the British Crown and various Māori chiefs in 1840. Page 76, J.B. Derbet, 'Overseers punishing slaves on a rural estate'. (3 vols., Paris, 1834,1835, 1839), Voyage Pittoresque et historique au Bresil. Page 82, Sir George Grey, by Sir Hubert von Herkomer (died 1914), given to the National Portrait Gallery, London in 1901. Page 83, Pōtatau Te Wherowhero, Waikato chief, Taken at the Marae of the Great Waikato people the Ngāti Māhanga tribe of Te Papa o Rotu. He became the first Māori king in 1858. Angas, George French 1822-1886: The New Zealanders Illustrated. London, Thomas McLean, 1847. Page 89, The assassination of Archduke heir of Austria and of the Duchess his wife in Sarajewo, Illustrated supplement of 'Le Petit Journal'. July 12, 1914. Page 93, Robert Edward Lee Statue, Charlottesville. Page 113, Map of the Earth made in 1893 by Orlando Ferguson of Hot Springs, South Dakota. Page 115 (lower) US Dept of Commerce. Page 116, Rijswijk, Netherlands (probably, 16th or 17th century). Page 118, Breakdown of the New Zealand flag referendum two, March 2016, by electorate. L. Mortensen, re-coloured by Brythones. Page 120, El Paso, Texas in 1886. Bird's Eye View of El Paso, El Paso County Texas, 1886. Lithographer unknown. Page 122, The Flags of a Free Empire, Showing the Emblems of British Empire Throughout the World, Mees, Arthur, 1850-1923.

For product information and technology assistance,
in Australia call **1300 790 853**;
in New Zealand call **0800 449 725**

For permission to use material from this text or product, please email **aust.permissions@cengage.com**

National Library of New Zealand Cataloguing-in-Publication Data
A catalogue record for this book is available from the National Library of New Zealand

ISBN: 978 017 041839 3

Cengage Learning Australia
Level 7, 80 Dorcas Street
South Melbourne, Victoria, Australia 3205

Cengage Learning New Zealand
Unit 4B Rosedale Office Park
331 Rosedale Road, Albany, North Shore 0632, NZ

For learning solutions, visit **cengage.co.nz**

Printed in Australia by Ligare Pty Ltd.
2 3 4 5 6 7 8 22 21 20 19 18

Contents

1 Vocabulary: Using context to decipher meaning

When reading a text where there are difficult words, it is a useful skill to be able to use the context – the rest of the sentence or nearby sentences – to help make an informed guess as to what the word means. It might be that a word you do know makes sense in the context and thus is probably a good alternative. Sometimes the difficult word is helpfully defined in the same sentence, or elsewhere in the text (many textbooks do this). Finally, the difficult word might be followed by words such as 'not', 'unlike' or similar that are good clues as to what a word does *not* mean. From this, you can deduce what it does mean.

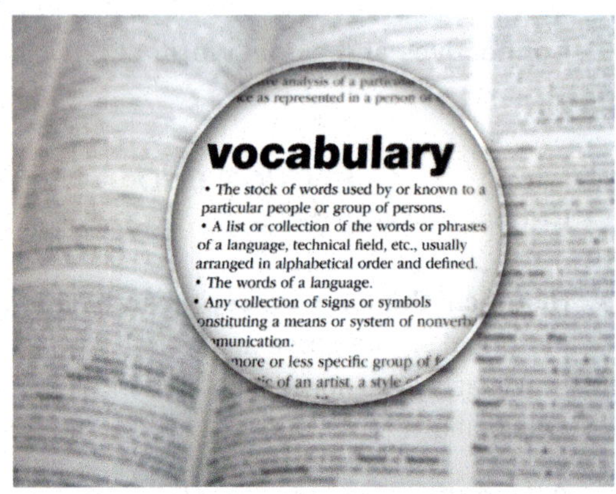

1 ACTIVITY

Try to determine the meanings of the following *vocabulary words*, based on the context clues in the sentences.

1 Angelo frequently showed *enmity* towards his classmates by throwing rubbish and shouting, but his sister Mariana was kind and quieter.

____

2 The little girl was showing signs of *opthalmic* problems – she squinted to read the whiteboard and complained of headaches after working on the computer for too long.

____

3 The crowd responded to the band with *plaudits* by clapping and cheering in high praise at the completion of their set.

____

4 Elena's *repudiation* of Hirini's bad manners was obvious to everyone at dinner as she dropped her napkin and left the table.

____

  ISBN: 9780170418393

5 From ancient times to the present day, the moon has been thought to cause *psychosis*. Some studies have shown that this momentary insanity does have some association with the moon's phases.

6 The old man's hair was *scant* rather than thick and full like it was when he was young.

7 Janie was a *pious* Muslim, regularly attending the mosque and prayer meetings.

8 My sister Mere has a great *abhorrence* of crowds, whereas my little brother Rawiri loves to be the centre of attention.

9 When you *admonish* someone, you point out their errors; an example would be telling off a child for misbehaving.

10 The sorcerer's *acolytes* watched carefully as he took them methodically through his spells.

11 Ninety-seven pairs is a *superfluous* number of shoes!

12 The spy was hung at the gallows of his homeland for his *perfidious* deeds.

13 'Scared to death' and 'quiet as a mouse' are *hackneyed* phrases – you see them far too often in student creative writing.

14 Amelia was as *ostentatious* as a spoilt princess when she arrived at the party. She tossed her coat to the hostess, ignored everyone and grabbed a drink out of a nearby guest's hand!

15 We always listen to my great-aunt because she is *venerable*, but we don't pay my niece too much attention as she's only fourteen.

2 ACTIVITY

In the activities below, a word from each sentence has been replaced with the 'non-word' *crangle*. Your task is to decide what *crangle* most likely means, based on the rest of the sentence and/or any clues you might be able to pick up from the other statements. You can give a single-word answer, or use several words.

Examples

1 The large red *crangle* fell from the tree and was quickly eaten by the goat below.
- In this case, the word is a noun and might be a type of fruit, such as an apple or plum.

2 She *crangled* her bicycle to school.
- In this case, the missing word is a verb and could be 'pedalled', 'rode', 'raced' or something similar.

1 Kate Sheppard and other campaigners quickly realised that their goal of *crangle* to alcohol laws would be best achieved if women got the vote.

2 Sheppard argued that women were not truly free without the vote, and that only full emancipation would finally give them this *crangle.*

3 In 1887, local franchise departments were formed and Sheppard was appointed overall *crangle* of the franchise and legislation departments nationwide.

4 In this position, she was *crangle* for co-ordinating and encouraging the local branches; she also ensured that information pamphlets were written and distributed, and members constantly wrote letters to the newspapers.

5 As leader of the franchise department, Sheppard ensured that all of its members had training and enough information to *crangle* the public 'about women's freedom and the influencing of legislation towards emancipation'.

6 Sheppard had a clear, logical intellect, and could also conduct an argument without bitterness. She was motivated by humanitarian *crangles* and a strong sense of justice: 'All that separates us – whether it be race, class, creed, or sex – is inhuman, and must be overcome.'

7 The emphasis throughout the campaign was on the right of women to vote; that right had earlier been *crangled* to males over 21 years but women, by being excluded, had been *crangled* along with others who could not vote: juveniles, lunatics and criminals. *(Two different words)*

8 Sheppard's franchise department took the first of three major *crangles* to Parliament in 1891. It was signed by more than 9000 women, and the second in 1892 by more than 19,000. The largest *crangle* ever presented to Parliament was collected in 1893 with nearly 32,000 signatures.

9 The Electoral Act 1893 was passed on 19 September and Kate Sheppard received a telegram from the premier, Richard Seddon (previously her political enemy in Parliament), *crangling* her and the women's suffrage movement for their victory.

10 It was 10 weeks before the *crangle*, and Sheppard and others set about enrolling women to vote; 65% of all New Zealand women over 21 voted in the 1893 *crangle*. New Zealand had become the first country in which all women *crangled* the right to vote. *(Two different words)*

ISBN: 9780170418393

2 First impressions: Skimming and scanning

Skimming

Skimming a text involves quickly getting a rough idea what it is about without actually reading it in detail. This process helps when there is a large amount of text and/or not much time to read it. This might be the case when locating sources that could be useful for an inquiry. After skimming and getting a general idea of what the text is about, closer reading of the text can follow where you further develop your initial understanding.

To quickly **skim** a text:

1. Read the title, subtitles and any subheadings first.
2. Read the first sentence (topic/key idea sentence) of each paragraph.
3. Read the last sentence (link sentence) of each paragraph.
4. If any other words in between 'jump out at you', note/highlight them.

Scanning

Scanning is different to skimming. When scanning you look *only* for specific facts or pieces of information, without reading everything. Scanning is thus more purposeful in that you already have an idea of the information you're looking for. During scanning you run your eyes quickly down a text looking for specific words (and/or numbers/dates, etc.) related to the topic you're interested in.

ISBN: 9780170418393

1 ACTIVITY

Skimming

Use the guidelines for skimming to provide a quick analysis of the key points in the text below. Do not directly copy any points; summarise them briefly in your own words. The reading part of this activity (skimming) should take only 60–90 seconds.

The changing role of Pakeha women in the 19th century

In the pre-Treaty 'contact period', 1790s–1840, most of the Pakeha women in New Zealand were the wives of Christian missionaries. These women were the 'glue' that held the mission stations together while the (male) missionaries were away travelling to distant Maori communities. Missionary wives fulfilled traditional roles, such as cooking and housekeeping, bearing and raising children, upholding Christian moral values, and also teaching in the mission schools (many learned te reo). They often had to endure many hardships, and the uncertainties associated with living among 'savages', especially as Maori initially viewed missionaries only as sources of trade.

With the signing of the Treaty in 1840 came an increasing number of settlers and their 'pioneer wives'. The early organisers of British settlements in New Zealand maintained that women had an all-important part to play in colonisation: to create and care for house and home, freeing men for the real work of breaking in the land for farming. Her duty was to guard the virtue, morality and civility of the settlers. Thus women's traditional roles after the Treaty remained much the same as those of the wives of missionaries. This included the bringing up and educating of children and contributing to the family economy, including raising poultry, milking and making butter, preserving fruit and other such chores. The historian Charlotte Macdonald has challenged the traditional stereotype of the heroic pioneer wife, pointing out that there was a common theme of 'unsettlement' in the lives of many women migrants, namely the problems facing women in a 'frontier society' such as loneliness, male alcoholism and violence, diseases, and problems with childbirth.

As the growing British population became more settled in the 1860s and 1870s, marriage was still the 'main occupation' of women. The 1874 census showed 15% of women over 20 were single and only 5% of those aged over 30. While single women did migrate to New Zealand during these two decades (many with financial assistance from the government), by 1891 the occupation of most women was still given as 'wife'. Even the role of household servant was seen as a preparation for women becoming true 'help-meets' for their husbands. Work patterns of New Zealand women reinforced emphasis on home and family; only 20% of women over the age of 15 worked outside the home in 1874, and 24% in 1891. (Of these, a growing number entered the light industrial workforce – particularly in clothing factories – during the Long Depression of the 1880s.) For women in the home, it is important to remember that life was not as frustrating in New Zealand as it

ISBN: 9780170418393

was in Britain. In the colonial context the role provided demands and challenges that held a high degree of personal reward, satisfaction, sense of purpose, a feeling of usefulness and greater independence.

With increased settlement and the transformation from a Maori country to a settler colony, by the late 19th century a middle class began to form and the wives of educated and/or successful colonists had time to address social issues. Such women were at the forefront of campaigns such as the temperance *[anti-alcohol]* and related female suffrage *[voting rights]* movements. Many (but not all) were unhappy that women were, in the historian Judith Malone's words, 'third-class citizens' in the eyes of the law. In areas such as divorce, pay rates, property, education, morality (the Contagious Diseases Act) and political and social rights, women were inferior. Traditional roles – the domestic sphere – remained. Changes did occur, beginning with the 1860 Married Women's Property Act and the subsequent 1884 amendment. In 1877 primary education was made compulsory for boys and girls. Political rights at a local body level were gradually granted and eventually, in 1893, women were enfranchised *[given the right to vote]*.

Adapted from Dalziel, Raewyn, 'The Colonial Helpmeet: Women's role and the vote in 19th Century New Zealand' in Brookes, B.; Macdonald, C.; Tennant, M. (eds), *Women in History: Essays on European Women in New Zealand*, Allen & Unwin/Port Nicholson Press, 1986.

Skimming: Text summary

ISBN: 9780170418393

2 ACTIVITY

Scanning

Scan the text on pages 8–9 quickly, this time looking only for the specific facts or pieces of information below, without reading everything. Briefly describe/explain the following.

1 'glue'

2 'unsettlement'

3 '15% of women over 20'

4 'third-class citizens'

3 ACTIVITY

Skimming

Use the guidelines for skimming to provide a quick analysis of the key points in the text on pages 10–12. Do not directly copy any points; summarise them briefly in your own words. The reading part of this activity (skimming) should take only 60–90 seconds. *(Note: the paragraph numbers and words in bold are not relevant to this activity.)*

'The Shrieking Sisterhood'

(1) The women who led the fight for women's suffrage were determined, strong-minded, committed to the cause and **articulate** in their arguments. Many people in New Zealand needed persuading that giving women the vote would not collapse the economy or society as a whole. The suffrage campaigners were well prepared to argue for the vote for women, and also knew how to effectively counter arguments against it. The campaigners were a new breed of women in a society that had traditionally **assigned** women to the roles of mother and housewife. Many men found them threatening and intimidating and

ISBN: 9780170418393

consequently heaped personal abuse and ridicule on their heads. Out of this **derision**, suffrage opponents coined the phrase 'The Shrieking Sisterhood' in an attempt to ridicule them. One can perhaps imagine that these women wore the **epithet** with some pride as ultimately they had the last word when the Electoral Bill was enacted on 19 September 1893, giving all women the vote in New Zealand. Many women made significant contributions to achieving this.

(2) Kate Sheppard is **synonymous** with New Zealand Women's Franchise. She worked tirelessly in her capacity as Franchise Superintendent of the Women's Christian Temperance Union to **champion** the cause of votes for women. She organised the three largest petitions presented to the House in 1891, 1892 and 1893 that finally secured the vote for women on 19 September 1893. She later went on to become the first President of the National Council of Women and carried on the fight for women's rights in New Zealand.

(3) Ada Wells dedicated her life to advancing equality for women in New Zealand and fighting to improve conditions for children and women. She was an active member of the women's suffrage movement in the late 1800s, and worked closely with Kate Sheppard on the WTCU **Enfranchisement** Committee. Ada went on to become the first Secretary of the newly formed National Council of Women as well as becoming the first woman to be elected to the Christchurch City Council, and the second woman to be appointed to a Charitable Aid Board.

(4) Margaret Sievwright was a shy, sensitive woman who worked passionately and selflessly to improve conditions for women in the colony. She first came to national prominence when she took on the demanding role as the Gisborne Leader of the Women's Christian Temperance Union and began to agitate not only for women's suffrage, but for vastly improved legal protections for women, in particular laws covering marriage and divorce, access to education, wages and working conditions, and matrimonial property. Margaret Sievwright was a founding member of the National Council of Women and she was elected President in 1901–02. She was again President in 1905 at the time of her death. Her knowledge of the law was extensive and one of the tributes paid to her on her death stated *'that her **acquaintance** with the laws relating to women were perhaps unequalled by any living woman'.*

(5) Amey Daldy has been variously described as 'uncompromising', 'stroppy', and 'not afraid to champion unpopular causes'. When Mary Leavitt arrived in New Zealand as an **envoy** for the American Women's Christian Temperance Union, Amey was immediately attracted to her cause of temperance. She had witnessed first-hand the destructiveness of alcohol abuse. Amey Daldy, along with other women in Auckland, initiated the formation of a WCTU branch in the city. From this she became actively involved in promoting social reform, better education opportunities for women and children, as well as pushing for women's suffrage. She worked with Annie Jane Schnackenberg and Kate Sheppard. In 1893 she resigned as Auckland Franchise Superintendent of the WCTU, because she was already holding the Founding President's role in the Auckland Women's Franchise League.

ISBN: 9780170418393

(6) Lady Anna Stout was a strong-minded woman who was fearless and outspoken in her views. At 18 she married Robert Stout, an MP and barrister in Dunedin. She quickly produced six children, which kept her fully occupied in the first years of her marriage. In 1885 she became a foundation member of the WCTU in Dunedin as well as in 1886 joining the New Zealand Alliance. These two organisations gave her the platform and opportunity to advocate her views on the advancement of women's rights and security. In 1892 she was elected as one of the two Presidents of the Dunedin Women's Franchise League. She campaigned tirelessly for suffrage. Not one to **rest on her laurels**, after suffrage was granted she continued to push for reforms on a wide number of issues. In 1895 she founded the Southern Cross Society for the purposes of securing education for all women irrespective of race or class. She was also elected one of the first Vice Presidents of the National Council of Women in 1896. She did not always see eye to eye with the Council and was never afraid of becoming **embroiled** in controversy. She criticised the National Council of Women for being too political and at one stage refused to attend their conference because the Council was not representative of all sections of the women's community.

(7) Marion Hatton became involved in the suffrage movement in her late fifties. She was one of the leaders of the Dunedin suffrage campaign. In April 1892 she chaired a large public meeting and the movement began to gain momentum. Shortly after this public meeting she **presided over** the formation of the Dunedin Women's Franchise League. She was duly elected its first President and in this capacity she spoke widely at public meetings and supported fellow campaign workers in collecting signatures for their Parliamentary petitions. After the vote was granted, Marion Hatton continued to pursue work that promoted women's interests and advanced the temperance cause. The Dunedin Women's Franchise League after 1893 expanded its work into providing social assistance to the less fortunate in Dunedin through soup kitchens and relief work. Marion Hatton also attended the **inaugural** meeting of the National Council of Women in 1896 and she was elected Vice President of the Council in 1898.

(8) Annie Jane Schnackenberg was one of New Zealand's leading feminists during the late 19th and early 20th century. In her early life in New Zealand she became involved in missionary work. It was during this phase of her life that she met and subsequently married Cort Schnackenberg in 1864. They had five children and continued to work in mission schools until Cort died in 1880. Annie returned to Auckland with her children and became attracted to the temperance *[anti-alcohol]* cause. In 1885 she joined the Auckland WCTU as a foundation member, and within this organisation she found a ready outlet for her Christian and moral beliefs. She strongly believed in social purity – a cause she was to pursue all her life. In 1891 Annie was elected National President of the WCTU. She remained President for the next decade, overseeing the securing of the vote and presiding over a huge celebratory public meeting in Auckland. In the remaining years of her life she fought for women's rights and improved **legislation** that guaranteed security for women. In particular, she campaigned hard for raising the age of consent, the repeal of the Contagious Diseases Act and prohibition.

Adapted from the Dictionary of New Zealand Biography, http://www.teara.govt.nz/en/biographies.

ISBN: 9780170418393

National Council of Women, Christchurch, 1896. From left, standing: Mrs A. Ansell (Dunedin), Mrs Henry Smith (Christchurch), Miss A. E. Hookham (Christchurch), Mrs G. Ross (Christchurch), Miss Jessie Mackay (Christchurch), Mrs Isherwood (Christchurch), Mrs Black (Christchurch), Mrs Widdowson (Christchurch), Miss F. Garstin (Christchurch), Mrs Wallis (Christchurch), Mrs Darling (Christchurch), Mrs J. M. Williamson (Wanganui), Mrs Wilson (Christchurch). Seated: Mrs G. J. Smith (Christchurch), Mrs A. Daldy (Auckland), Mrs Hatton (Dunedin; Vice President), Lady Anna Stout (Wellington; Vice President), Mrs Kate Sheppard (Christchurch; President), Mrs A. J. Schnackenberg (Auckland; Vice President), Mrs W. Sievwight (Gisborne), Mrs M. A. Tasker (Wellington), Mrs D. Izett (Christchurch; Secretary). Seated on floor: Mrs C. M. Alley (Malvern), Mrs A. Wells (Christchurch), Miss Bain (Christchurch).

Skimming: Text summary

Scanning

Scan the text on pages 10–12 quickly, looking only for the specific facts or pieces of information below, without reading everything. Briefly describe/explain the following. *(Note: the paragraph numbers and words in bold are not relevant to this activity.)*

1 '**The Shrieking Sisterhood**'.

2 The first woman elected to the **Christchurch City Council**.

3 What **Amey Daldy** did in **1893**.

4 The purpose of the **Southern Cross Society**.

5 The year that **Cort** and **Annie Jane Schnackenberg** were married.

ISBN: 9780170418393

5 ACTIVITY

Decoding difficult vocabulary

Use the context around the words in **bold** in the text on pages 10–12 to explain briefly and as best you can what they mean. (You may already know the meaning of some or even many of these words; nevertheless, do check the context to ensure that your understanding is specific to this text.) If you cannot work these out, use a dictionary and then check the definition against the context of the sentence in which the word is used.

1 Paragraph 1: **articulate**

2 Paragraph 1: **assigned**

3 Paragraph 1: **derision**

4 Paragraph 1: **epithet**

5 Paragraph 2: **synonymous**

6 Paragraph 2: **champion**

7 Paragraph 3: **enfranchisement**

ISBN: 9780170418393

8 Paragraph 4: **acquaintance**

9 Paragraph 5: **envoy** (Confirm your answer for **6** 'champion' as well.)

10 Paragraph 6: **rest on her laurels**

11 Paragraph 6: **embroiled**

12 Paragraph 7: **presided over**

13 Paragraph 7: **inaugural**

14 Paragraph 8: **legislation**

ISBN: 9780170418393

3 Connectives and signal words

As you study a source there are certain types of words that can help signal a relationship between ideas. Recognising such words can help you quickly skim through a text. You can also refer to this list when you are writing your own responses or essays.

Relationship	Connecting word(s)
Introduction	the topic/issue/study area; this report, my purpose/questions/area of interest/hypothesis
Describing procedures or time sequences	the first step, to begin with, initially, before, at this point, secondly, subsequently, following this step, next, then, meanwhile, after that, after a while, later, finally, consequently
Giving example	for example, for instance, including, such as, another reason, another example, can be illustrated by, as follows
Comparing	both ... and ..., similarly, in most cases, not only ... but also ..., more, most, less, least, less than, more than
Contrasting	but, however, on the other hand, in contrast to, whereas, alternatively, is different from, differs from, on the contrary, although, yet, nevertheless, despite this
Adding information	also, as well as, another point, another factor, another reason, in addition, additionally, besides, furthermore, moreover
Cause and effect	due to, because of, the reason for, consequently, in that case, hence, as a result of, as a consequence of, since, the effect of, if ... then ..., therefore, stemmed from, an outcome of, accordingly
Interpreting data	as can be seen by, according to, as shown in, evidence indicates, as exemplified by, as a result of
Conclusion	in conclusion, thus, therefore, for these reasons, these points lead to, as a result, the results indicate, accordingly, to summarise

From *Effective Literacy Strategies in Years 9–13*, p. 169.

ISBN: 9780170418393

In *The Big Six Historical Thinking Concepts*, Dr Peter Seixas and Tom Morton write that learning to apply historical skills and concepts works best when it is done to foster a disposition or 'habit of mind'. What this means is that when we read sources, be they primary or secondary, we will *automatically* apply some or all of the historical skills and concepts. This is not the same as learning and applying them 'mechanically', like a checklist: it is *a way of thinking* that will eventually become automatic. We thus should not worry so much about there being 'right' and 'wrong' interpretations but focus instead on coming up with our own interpretations based on the evidence as we understand it.

The 'Big Six' historical thinking concepts

1 Establish historical significance
2 Use/analyse primary source evidence (close reading)
3 Identify continuity and change
4 Analyse cause and consequence
5 Analyse historical perspectives
6 Understand the ethical dimension of historical interpretations

In this workbook we will focus on the first four concepts, plus look at some other equally important historical relationships.

How historical evidence is 'created'

A An event of some sort occurs and an artefact *[item/object]* comes into existence.

B The artefact survives and is preserved over time. This could be intentionally, as in an archive or in someone's possession, or it could be simply by good luck.

C The artefact is later discovered by someone who thinks it is important enough to study further.

D The artefact is evaluated using a range of historians' skills. Other relevant primary and secondary sources are also taken into account. Through this evaluation process the artefact has now been transformed into historical evidence.

E This evidence, and other evidence like it, is collated into a 'historical narrative' (often in the form of a history book or article).

  ISBN: 97801703XXXXX

4 Historical thinking concept: Establishing historical significance

The past is big. It is everything that has ever happened to anyone anywhere. There is way too much history to study or remember it all. Choices must be made about what is deemed worth remembering and what is not. This is where the concept of 'significance' comes in.

1 ACTIVITY

Individual activity

1 On the timeline below, write in what you think have been the SIX most significant events in your life to date.

I was born

2 Explain what criteria *[reasoning]* you used when making judgments about the significance of each of the six events. In your thinking, you can also consider why you decided NOT to include many of the other events in your life.

Event 1: ______________________________

Event 2: ______________________________

Event 3: ______________________________

Critical thinking skills

ISBN: 9780170418393

Event 4: ______________________________

____

Event 5: ______________________________

____

Event 6: ______________________________

____

2 ACTIVITY

Group activity

1 On the timeline below, write in what you think have been the SIX most significant events in your group's SCHOOL life to date.

We started school

2 Explain what criteria *[reasoning]* your group used when making judgments about the significance of each of the six events. In your thinking, you can also consider why as a group you decided NOT to include here many of the other events in your school life.

Event 1: ______________________________

____

Event 2: ______________________________

____

Event 3: ______________________________

____

Event 4: ______________________________

____

Event 5: ______________________________

____

Event 6: ______________________________

____

 ISBN: 9780170418393

3 Discuss and note down any issues you had in agreeing on what was significant enough to include.

4 How might this exercise be relevant to the craft of writing history?

What makes something 'historically significant'?

Seixas and Morton state that significant events include those that resulted in great change over long periods of time for large numbers of people. A historical person or event can also acquire significance if historians can link them or it to larger trends and stories that reveal something important for us today. Naturally, historians will not necessarily agree on the relative significance of events/people. This is healthy and it forces us to think carefully about the evidence used to support the different perspectives. It is important to note that 'It is significant because it is in the history book' and 'It is significant because I am interested in it' are inadequate explanations of historical significance.

Historical significance: Achievement Standard criteria

The notion of 'historical significance' is further developed in the relevant Achievement Standards' Explanatory Notes. Here it is stated that significance is a concept that is typically determined by some or all of the following criteria:

- the importance of the event to people alive at the time
- how deeply people's lives were affected at the time
- how many lives were affected
- the length of time people's lives were affected
- the extent to which the event continues to affect society.

3 ACTIVITY

Brief summaries are provided below of two key historical events.

1 Your first task is to complete the vocabulary activities, referring to the words in bold in the text.

2 Your next job is to refer to some or all of the 'Historical significance' criteria above and evidence from the text to justify which event you think is more significant than the other.
   - For the purpose of this activity, you cannot say that they are equally significant. (Historians would probably disagree with you anyway.)
   - You may write down your evidence and/or highlight it directly in the text.

3 When finished, discuss your views and evidence with others in the class.

EVENT 1a

World War I: The war fought between 28 July 1914 and 11 November 1918 was known at the time as the Great War and the 'War to End All Wars'. Only when the world went to war again in the 1930s and '40s did the earlier conflict become known as the First World War. Its **casualty** totals were **unprecedented**, with around 17 million killed and another 20 million wounded, far outstripping anything seen before. Lethal new technologies were unleashed and, for the first time, a major war was fought not only on land and on sea but below the sea and in the skies as well. The two sides were known as the Allies – consisting primarily of France, Great Britain, Italy, Russia and, later, the United States – and the Central Powers, primarily Austria-Hungary (the Habsburg Empire), Germany, and the Ottoman Empire (Turkey). A number of smaller nations aligned themselves with one side or the other. The Allies were the victors, as the entry of the United States into the war in 1917 added an additional weight of men and **materiel**, such as artillery, transport and machine guns, which the Central Powers could not hope to match. The war resulted in a dramatically changed **geo-political landscape**, including the destruction of three empires: Austro-Hungarian, Ottoman and Russian. New borders were drawn at its conclusion and resentments, especially on the part of Germany, remained **festering** in Europe to later re-emerge as a significant cause of the Second World War. From 2014 to 2018 commemorations of main events in the war occurred worldwide. In some countries, such as New Zealand and Australia, Anzac Day is commemorated every year with large crowds in attendance.

Adapted from http://www.historynet.com/world-war-i.

EVENT 1b

World War II: The **primary combatants** were the Axis nations (**comprising** Nazi Germany, fascist Italy, Imperial Japan and their smaller allies) and the Allied nations, led by Britain (and its Commonwealth nations), the Union of Soviet Socialist Republics and the United States of America. The Allies were the victors. Two superpowers, the USA and USSR, emerged from World War II to begin a Cold War with each other that would define much of the rest of the century. The exact cost in human lives is unknown, but casualties in World War II may have totalled 55 million killed, many of them **non-combatants** unable to escape the destruction of their homes in towns and cities. The Second World War brought about major leaps in technology and laid the groundwork that permitted postwar social changes. These included the end of **European colonialism**, as European powers granted independence (willingly or not) to countries in Africa and Asia. In the United States the civil rights movement **incrementally** gained greater equality in law throughout the 1950s and '60s. The modern women's rights movement made similar progress in the 1970s and '80s. As well as social changes, technological advancements led to missile technology and programmes for exploring outer space.

Adapted from http://www.historynet.com/world-war-ii.

ISBN: 9780170418393

Task 1: Vocabulary

Use the context to explain briefly the meaning of the following words **bolded** in the *EVENT 1a* text, page 22 (you may provide a single-word synonym if you can).

1 casualty ____________________

____

2 unprecedented ____________________

____

3 materiel *(note the unusual spelling)* ____________________

____

4 geo-political landscape ____________________

____

5 festering ____________________

____

Task 2: Vocabulary

Use the context to explain briefly the meaning of the following words **bolded** in the *EVENT 1b* text, page 22 (you may provide a single-word synonym if you can).

1 primary combatants ____________________

____

2 comprising ____________________

____

3 non-combatants ____________________

____

4 European colonialism ____________________

____

5 incrementally ____________________

____

Task 3: Evaluation of significance

- The event that I think is more significant is: World War I/World War II. *(Circle one)*
- Your justification. (Which criteria from page 21 best apply? What evidence from the text supports your view?)

____

____

____

____

____

____

- Discuss your response with others in the class.

ISBN: 9780170418393

EVENT 2a

Russian Revolution: The Russian Revolution that brought the Soviet Union into existence after 1917 generated a totally new way of thinking about the economy, society and the government. The victorious Bolsheviks had set out to cure Russia of all its deep injustices that arose from social class differences and inequality. The revolution marked the end of a **dynasty** that had lasted 300 years, replacing the Romanov Tsar (Emperor) with a Council of People's Commissars *[representatives]*. Private ownership of land, factories and other means of producing wealth were abolished and replaced by State ownership. Meanwhile, although in the early 20th century only a relatively small number of countries were capitalist democracies, they were powerful countries and among them was a **fervently** held belief that their way of ordering the world was the only **viable** one. After 1917 the **ideology** of communism seemed to present an equally workable alternative and, as communist ideas began to spread elsewhere, these capitalist countries were frightened. Some historians argue that Britain and France quietly preferred the rise of Hitler in the 1930s as a strong **bulwark** against the spread of Russian communism, thus **tacitly** encouraging and emboldening him. When China became communist in 1949 at the beginning of what would become known as the Cold War, around 1.5 billion of the world's population of 4.5 billion were under communist rule.

EVENT 2b

Cold War: The term 'Cold War' was **coined** by the British author George Orwell after World War II. He used it to describe a postwar 'peace that is no peace' where the ideological tension between the two superpowers (USA and Russia) had the clear **potential** for global nuclear war. The military capacity developed during the Cold War was an enormously costly and dangerous means of 'keeping the peace'. Each side had a **surfeit** of weapons, far more than were needed for self-defence. At their peak, the world's nuclear stockpiles held 18 billion tons of explosive energy. The total cost of the Cold War has been estimated at US$8 trillion. Although nuclear war never did break out, it came very close on several occasions, notably in the Cuban Missile Crisis in 1962. The Cold War still cost millions of lives in '**proxy wars**' such as those in Korea, Vietnam and Afghanistan where the superpowers backed 'their' side but did not directly fight each other. The Cold War also destroyed free thought and all manner of other freedoms in communist countries, where paranoid leaders believed that unapproved ideas would **jeopardise** their power. This was also seen to a limited extent in the USA (and elsewhere) during the 'Great Fear' of the 1950s. Overall, the collapse of communism in Europe in 1990 had little impact on the global economy. This shows that communism had in fact failed to provide a **feasible** alternative to capitalism, at least in terms of generating wealth.

Task 1: Vocabulary

Use the context to explain briefly the meaning of the following words **bolded** in the *EVENT 2a* text (you may provide a single-word synonym if you can).

1 dynasty ______________________________

____

 ISBN: 9780170418393

2 fervently

3 viable

4 ideology

5 bulwark

6 tacitly

Task 2: Vocabulary

Use the context to explain briefly the meaning of the following words **bolded** in the *EVENT 2b* text (you may provide a single-word synonym if you can).

1 coined

2 potential

3 surfeit

4 'proxy wars'

5 jeopardise

6 feasible

Task 3: Evaluation of significance

- The event that I think is more significant is: Russian Revolution/Cold War. *(Circle one)*
- Your justification. (Which criteria from page 21 best apply? What evidence from the text supports your view?)

- Discuss your response with others in the class.

ISBN: 9780170418393

EVENT 3a

New Zealand Wars: The main phase of the series of **geographically disparate** conflicts known collectively as the New Zealand Wars took place between 1859 and 1872 across a wide **swathe** of the central North Island. The key battles took place in Taranaki, Waikato and near Tauranga, but it was the Waikato campaigns that most severely **compromised** Maori military resistance. Historian James Cowan estimates total Maori losses at just over 2000 killed and an unknown number wounded. Government forces, including a number of 'friendly' Maori, suffered around 600 killed. In addition, the Waikato tribes had around 1,000,000 acres of land confiscated by the government. Economically, the Waikato tribes were devastated and trade virtually ceased. Disease and food shortages plagued the **exiles** who fled to the hill country in neighbouring Ngati Maniapoto territory, which remained hostile to the government for some years. As Ngapora Tamati said in 1872: 'If the blood of our people only had been spilled, and the land remained, then this trouble would have been over long ago.' For settlers, however, the wars of the 1860s mostly settled the issue of who was to be the **sovereign power** in New Zealand, allowing progress to occur **unhindered** by Maori reluctance to sell land. Settlers could now convert the landscape and economy from a Maori one that had contained growing pockets of settlers to a fully Europeanised one. The Waikato tribes continued to seek redress from the government for what they saw as illegal confiscations. Finally, in 1995 a Waitangi Tribunal settlement package was agreed to, with the Crown acknowledging that 'the confiscations were wrongful and totally unjustified ... Waikato-Tainui, far from being in rebellion, were in fact defending hearth and home ... The Waikato war and the confiscations that followed caused devastation ... The people were dispersed, and there was widespread suffering, distress and deprivation ... The land of their ancestors had been taken from them with the stroke of a pen.'

EVENT 3b

Native Lands Act: The war in the Waikato and Taranaki in the 1860s had **decimated** Maori military resistance in the central North Island but it had not fully destroyed Maori **autonomy** there; a mostly independent territory existed in Ngati Maniapoto lands. However, where war had not entirely achieved the government's goals, the laws that followed did. The most far-reaching of these were the Native Lands Acts, the first of which was passed in 1862 establishing the Native Land Court. The purpose of the Court was to convert communal Maori ownership of land into individual ownership. The government claimed that doing so was in the best interest of Maori, helping them **assimilate** into the Pakeha world by forcing them to farm their land individually. In reality, no real assistance was given to Maori to transition to Pakeha-like farming methods. Making things worse for Maori were the traditional inter-hapu *[inter-tribal]* rivalries that were **litigated** in the Court, to the benefit of Pakeha **land speculators** looking to profit themselves. Any hapu with an interest in a piece of land would have to attend Court or lose all rights to it. Legal and surveying costs, and expenses associated with attending an often-distant Court, were very high. Even a hapu with a successful claim would often end up selling the land to pay off debts. Between 1872 and 1900, some eight million acres of land shifted into Pakeha ownership. By 1939, only about 3.5 million acres out of the North Island's 29.6 million acres remained in Maori ownership. No Maori community in the North Island was unaffected by the Native Lands Acts, and few institutions created by the Crown have had a more **pernicious** impact on Maori society.

 ISBN: 9780170418393

Task 1: Vocabulary

Use the context to explain briefly the meaning of the following words **bolded** in the *EVENT 3a* text (you may provide a single-word synonym if you can).

1 geographically disparate

2 swathe

3 compromised

4 exiles

5 sovereign power

6 unhindered

Task 2: Vocabulary

Use the context to explain briefly the meaning of the following words **bolded** in the *EVENT 3b* text (you may provide a single-word synonym if you can).

1 decimated

2 autonomy

3 assimilate

4 litigated

5 land speculators

6 pernicious

Task 3: Evaluation of significance

- The event that I think is more significant is: New ZealandWars/Native Lands Acts. *(Circle one)*
- Your justification. (Which criteria from page 21 best apply? What evidence from the text supports your view?)

- Discuss your response with others in the class.

EVENT 3c

Treaty of Waitangi: The Treaty was signed in 1840 between William Hobson, representative of the British Crown on the one hand, and over 500 chiefs, including 13 women on the other. Only 39 Maori signed an English copy. Although there would be differences in understanding, both sides wanted to ensure that the growing lawlessness would **desist** while trade would continue. The Treaty thus attempted to provide a foundation for a relationship between the two **parties**, and Maori likely understood that while this would mean some sort of power-sharing relationship they would still be mostly free to **exercise** their authority (rangatiratanga) as they had always done. For its part, the Crown believed that it had secured its sole authority in New Zealand. On this basis settlers began to trickle in; by the 1860s and even more so the 1870s this trickle had turned into a flood. While the new settlers thought little of the Treaty, Maori held fast to it, more so as they began to be **marginalised** in their own land: by 1910 they held just 1% of the South Island and 27% of the North; the settler population exceeded 750,000 while the Maori population was around 45,000. Although Maori no longer had any meaningful political authority they refused to let the Treaty die. After many decades of **reproaching** the government for its failure to honour the Treaty, a series of increasingly vocal protest actions, along with quieter political action behind the scenes, began to bring about change. The establishment of the Waitangi Tribunal in 1975 (along with its greater powers in 1985) was a step forward. Today, while the Treaty is recognised formally in only some laws, it does carry, according to the Treaty Resource Centre, 'considerable **moral force** based on the honour of the Crown'.

ISBN: 9780170418393

Task 4: Vocabulary

Use the context to explain briefly the meaning of the following words **bolded** in the *EVENT 3c* text (you may provide a single-word synonym if you can).

1 desist ______________________________

____

2 parties ______________________________

____

3 exercise ______________________________

____

4 marginalised ______________________________

____

5 reproaching ______________________________

____

6 moral force ______________________________

____

Task 5: Evaluation of significance

- The event that I think is more significant is: my choice from Task 3/Treaty of Waitangi (page 28). *(Circle one)*
- Your justification. (Which criteria from page 21 best apply? What evidence from the text supports your view?)

____

____

____

____

____

____

- Discuss your response with others in the class.

ISBN: 9780170418393

5 Asking questions of a source

When a historian studies a source, especially a primary one, frequently more questions than answers will be generated in his or her mind. Not only will these questions provide direction for seeking further information, but they will also help them critically evaluate the source. This is high-level thinking in action. Matthew H. Bowker, Assistant Professor of Interdisciplinary Studies at Medaille College *[University]* in Buffalo, New York, teaches courses in political science, philosophy, critical thinking, and undergraduate research and writing. One of his key areas of research is the important role of asking questions:

> Philosophers, cognitive scientists, anthropologists, and psychologists have argued convincingly that the act of questioning is central to thinking, to storing and communicating knowledge … Requiring students to create their own questions helps them understand how the answers we have come to accept are connected, contingent *[inter-dependent]* and contextual; how they rely on, imply, and beg additional questions. In this question-centred pedagogy *[learning approach]* the questions themselves are the answers. Our capacity to generate answers is often less important than our ability to interrogate the answers we already have. Learning answers without learning questions produces a kind of ideology in which everything is already settled … everything 'is what it is' and nothing more need be known.

Closer to home, Rachel Morris, a New Zealand-born journalist working for *Huffington Post*'s online magazine *Highline*, is clear about the value not only of the study of History, but its important role in developing a questioning mind: 'Studying History is really good preparation for journalism. You learn to track down obscure information, write clearly, evaluate different sources, and weigh up multiple versions of the same event. Above all, you figure out how to ask good questions.'

In recognition of the value of asking questions, in recent years the resource-based exam papers have given guidance on how students can demonstrate Excellence-level skills when analysing a source; among the pointers is: 'if appropriate, note relevant question(s) that the sources might raise in a historian's mind, which the historian might wish to investigate further.'

Exemplar: Asking questions

Alongside the text on page 31 is a sample of the sort of questions that might be raised in the mind of a historian as they carefully read this account. As noted above, it might not be easy to answer the questions but just asking shows engagement with the source, as well as providing direction for further research. Use these examples to guide your own questions on the remaining section of this text.

Note: You do not necessarily need to come up with as many questions as there are below, but also don't feel limited by the requirements of the task which asks for a minimum of only two or three questions.

ISBN: 9780170418393

Text 1: Wakefield and the signing of the Treaty of Waitangi

This (adapted) account is by Edward Wakefield, nephew of the founder of a British-based land-buying company called the New Zealand Company. Wakefield is in New Zealand to assist with the purchase of large amounts of land from Maori, on which British settlements will be established. This account was published in 1845, five years after the signing of the Treaty of Waitangi. The Treaty would put an end to the direct purchase of land from Maori; the Crown, represented by Governor Hobson, retained for itself the sole right to buy land from Maori. Here Wakefield recalls the arrival of two missionaries in a Maori settlement near Whanganui, bringing with them a copy of the Treaty for signing by the chiefs.

While I was waiting for the return of the chief Kuru and the gathering of the clans *[tribes]*, the missionaries Williams and Hadfield arrived by land. They held no communication with me; but I heard from the natives, and also from MacGregor, the skipper, who called upon them in their tent, what had been their proceedings. Turoa and Te Aratia, with several other of the chiefs who had held communication with them, told me that Mr Williams had asked them to sign a paper *[the Treaty]* and promised them a present of a blanket from the Queen.

They had answered at first by requesting Williams to show the paper *[Treaty]* to the other white people then on the spot, in order that the transaction should be a public one; which he had refused to do. He then asked them who the white people in the ship were; and upon their informing him that it was Wakefield and his land-buying party, he had urged them not to sell their land, saying that 'all the goods in the vessel were light, and might be lifted with the hand, but that the oneone, or land, could not.' They took care to assure me, however, that this bangareka or 'joke' of Williams, as they termed it, had not shaken their resolution of abiding by their decision to sell the agreed piece of land.

Questions this text might raise:

- It seems Wakefield knows the local iwi well. How long had he been there? What were the 'clans' gathering for?
- Was overland the usual way to travel? How difficult was it to travel this way? Where had they come from?
- What was MacGregor and his ship doing there? Trading? If so, was this common?
- Why would a blanket be offered as a gift? Was this a desirable item for Maori? If so, why?
- Wouldn't offering a gift be like a bribe to sign?
- How did the Europeans and Maori communicate? Had they learned each other's language?
- Did Turoa and Te Aratia know about the Queen? If so, how?
- Could Maori read?
- Was the Treaty in Maori or English?
- Why wouldn't Williams show the other 'white people' the Treaty?
- Why did Williams warn Maori not to sell their land to Wakefield? Does this affect how much we can trust Wakefield's version of the events given here?
- Is Williams right in his claim that Maori were not getting enough goods/payment for their land? If so, wouldn't it have been in Wakefield's interest not to tell us this bit in his account?
- How long had land purchases been going on? How extensive were they? It seems here that Maori were willing sellers. Is this the case everywhere?
- When did the settlers arrive?

Critical thinking skills

CLOSE READING ACTIVITY

Asking questions of a text

As you read the remainder of this account, note down any questions that occur to you. You can use the '5W, 1H' starters if this helps. There are no 'right' or 'wrong' questions, but 'Why' and 'How' questions tend to be higher level. Try to ask at least two or three questions per paragraph. When completed, share your questions with others in the class.

- Repeat this activity with Text 2 (page 33), Text 3 (page 34) and Text 4 (page 35).

In the evening of the day after Mr Williams' arrival, Turoa and Te Aratia came on board our vessel, and told me that they had received a blanket each on signing, and that Williams had departed to the southward. I could not ascertain *[find out]* whether any other chiefs had signed or not. I gathered from MacGregor that the paper was one ceding *[giving]* sovereignty to the Queen, similar to that to which the adhesion *[agreement]* of the Port Nicholson chiefs had been obtained. I was rather surprised that Mr Williams had not taken pains to acquire the assent *[agreement]* of more of the chiefs, or of any of those towards Patea and the country to the north.

On inquiring of Turoa whether he understood what he had signed, he repeated to me that my Queen had sent him a blanket, and that he had been told to make a mark in order to show that he had got it. When I explained to him that my Queen had become his also, and that she and her Governor were now chiefs over him as well as over me, he became very agitated, and repeatedly spoke of following Williams in order to return the blanket and upbraid *[scold]* him for the deception. He finally determined, however, that he must have got to Wanganui by that time, and that he could not catch him. 'But,' said he, 'a blanket is no payment for my name. I am still a chief.'

 ISBN: 9780170418393

Text 2: Traders and Maori

John Logan Campbell arrived in New Zealand in March 1840. He spent his initial time with the American William Webster (called Wepiha by Maori) on the Thames side of the Coromandel peninsula at his trading base at a place called Herekino. Later, he would purchase Motukorea (Browns Island) in Auckland's Hauraki Gulf, establishing his own trading base there. His account here was published in 1881.

Wepiha was a big man: he was, though a Yankee *[American]*, as burly as a veritable John Bull *['typical' strong Englishman]*. He was not only big in body but also in brain … Wepiha had found himself with a wife – native fashion, rather than in the church – from the tribe of the great chief Taniwha, who had three hundred – I don't mean wives, but fighting men. Under the shadow of the great Taniwha … lived and 'reigned' Wepiha. But Wepiha ruled not through his strength but through the power of two words, and throughout his dominions no two words were more often repeated by Maori than these: *whare hoko [trading house]*. Wepiha's strength lay in a modest-looking little building in one corner of Herekino beach – his *whare hoko*. Yes, it was for the contents of Wepiha's store that the natives were intensely loyal!

Tell me not of missionaries as civilising agents compared to a *whare hoko*. The poor missionary could only raise on high his Bible and threaten the casting out into darkness, which the Maori in his early days of childhood had not yet learned to fear. But Wepiha, if a tribe offended him, simply shut the door of his *whare hoko* in their faces; he forbid sale of his blankets and guns, his calico *[cloth]* and spades, his cotton prints and tomahawks. It was terrible enough to have to stand this dire punishment, but when there was also included the ambrosial weed *[tobacco]* and the clay pipe, human nature could stand it no longer, and the offenders humbly asked for pardon at the *whare hoko* door of Herekino that they might again be admitted … and be at peace with its master.

Although Wepiha was a king of his own creation, he nevertheless did pay a small tribute – a sort of blackmail on the sly – to his father-in-law, who, in consideration of permitting his daughter to remain Mrs Wepiha, periodically visited Herekino whenever his stock of tobacco ran low, or he had broken his clay pipe …

ISBN: 9780170418393

Text 3: A newly arrived settler at Wellington

Sarah Stephens arrived from England at the new settlement of Wellington on the Fifeshire in January 1842. Her husband, Samuel Stephens, a surveyor with the New Zealand Company, had arrived in September 1841. Mrs Duffy and Mrs Pointer were also going to join their husbands in Nelson. Both Wellington and Nelson (as well as Whanganui and New Plymouth) were settlements established by the New Zealand Company.

Sarah Stephens' journal letter to her sister
Wellington, 23 January 1842

When I had dressed in the morning I went on deck to see what I could of the great town of Wellington with which I must say I was not much impressed. A great number of folks came out from the shore to see what was to be seen and to hear what news from home was to be heard on our ship.

[The following day Sarah goes on shore.] As we landed we saw two of the natives squatting with their blankets, their faces were much tattooed. They looked so pleasant and held out their hands to shake ours which several of us did. To me all that was interesting in this place was connected with the natives. What has been said of them, as far as I can judge, is not one bit more than they deserve. They are a fine race of people and there is a great deal of intelligence in their countenances *[faces]*. All that we met were covered with a blanket or mat. The women I saw were not, generally speaking, so good looking as the men but the upper part of the face and eyes of the two with whom I spoke might be called handsome. They were more pleased with the white ladies than the gentlemen; the latter *[last-mentioned]* were frequently told by them that they were 'no good'. They can say and understand many English words and are fond of having a chat in their way. We made quite a gathering at the inn where we ended up. Mrs Duffy with Mrs Pointer and myself sitting on chairs and on the floor close by us one of the chiefs with his wife and her sister squatting with their blankets round them.

ISBN: 9780170418393

Text 4: 'The Wairau Affray'

The Wairau Affray (called a 'massacre' by the settlers) took place in Marlborough on 17 June 1843 when Nelson magistrate Henry Thompson, Captain Arthur Wakefield (uncle of Edward Wakefield) and an armed party of Nelson settlers set out to arrest Te Rauparaha for his followers' opposition to a survey of disputed land in the Wairau Valley. Twenty-two Pakeha, including Thompson and Arthur Wakefield, were killed, as were about six Maori. The new Governor, Robert FitzRoy, to intense settler indignation, upheld the Maori case over the disputed land and criticised the armed settlers for causing the quarrel with the Maori.

The official William Spain was appointed by the British government in 1841 to investigate land claims and titles in the colony. George Clarke, a former missionary, had in 1841 accepted the post, created by Governor Hobson, of Protector of Aborigines ['Aborigines' means 'native peoples'].

Letter from Mary Swainson to her grandparents in England
Wellington, 11 July 1843

Mr Thomson is (or rather was) a very violent man ... The natives, I ought to say, entreated *[pleaded]* that there should be no fighting as they were quite willing to wait until Mr Spain and Mr Clarke came, and they had a 'korero' (talk) about it, and that they would be quite content with what ruling they made about it ... There is not the least fear of the natives attacking us here, but as a proper precaution the Wellington settlers have now established a Militia *[armed settler organisation]*.

I only intended to remain a week here before heading home but there were several little gaieties *[fun events]* going on and the Colonel and Emily Wakefield pressed me very much to remain – so I did. The ship the *North Star* was in, which made the place rather happier than usual – particularly after that melancholy *[sad]* affair at Cloudy Bay *[i.e. 'The Wairau Affray']* which must continue to throw a dampness over us all here. Although no person belonging here was killed, what will be thought of it in England? The great 'dampener' here is the land claims being unsettled, and this Cloudy Bay business has made it even more so, for the Governor has issued a proclamation saying that all land disputed by the natives is to be left in their possession until the land claims are investigated. This has made the natives claim more than they ever did before, and consequently left the question in a worse state than ever – at least for the time being.

A similar process can be used when examining other types of sources, such as cartoons, photographs, posters, and so on. For more on this, see the *History Skills for NCEA Level 1* workbook.

Critical thinking skills

6 Historical thinking concept: Using/analysing primary source evidence (close reading)

You probably know by now that historians are totally dependent on primary sources to do their work. Primary sources are those produced by people who were around at the time of the events/period that the historians are interested in. Primary sources are like the pieces of a jigsaw puzzle, or the raw ingredients for a recipe. Historians use their skills and training to turn these sources into something useful – a historical analysis of the past (see also 'How historical evidence is "created"', page 18). These skills include the ability to think critically about the sources they use.

Each historian, including you, will approach a source with a different set of experiences and skills, and will therefore interpret the source differently. Remember that there is no one right interpretation. However, if you do not do a careful and thorough job, you can certainly arrive at a wrong interpretation.

Below are some of the thinking steps historians use as they analyse sources from the past. (If you have used *History Skills for NCEA Level 1*, you will be aware of the '5W, 1H' questioning approach to primary source analysis. The guidelines given here are a variation of that approach.)

Remember: Don't be overwhelmed by all the possible questions below; even a qualified historian might not be able to answer all or even many of them. The good news is that just asking questions of a source and thinking about them is part of the 'habit of mind' that Seixas and Morton talked about in *The Big Six Historical Thinking Concepts* as being the mark of a critical thinker. (See page 18.)

Critical thinking questions: 'CAP' analysis

The guidelines below will help you analyse a source to determine its usefulness, as well as reliability and any limitations.

Confirmation?

As noted above, each piece of primary evidence is like part of a jigsaw puzzle. Just like you wouldn't try to predict what the whole picture is from a few pieces of a puzzle, historians also avoid trying to 'predict' the past from a limited range of evidence. The more primary evidence there is from different perspectives, the better!

1. Does all the primary evidence we have tell a similar story? And if not, why not?
2. Why/how did this source survive in the historical record?
3. As well as the viewpoints/voices that we *are* hearing through the primary evidence, whose viewpoints/ voices are *missing*, and why is this so? What might their views/experiences have been?

ISBN: 9780170418393

Author

A key question historians ask of the primary evidence is: Who *created* it?

1 What do we know about the author?
- What is their race, sex, class, occupation, religion, age, region, political beliefs?
- Does any of this matter? If so, how?

2 What were the times like in which the author lived? (Knowing the values system in place for the author, and whether or not they accepted them, can help us better understand the source.)
- For example, was slavery considered 'normal'? Was the 'proper' place for women considered to be in the home? Was everyone theoretically equal, as under communism?

3 Did the person who created the evidence/source actually witness the events themselves?
- If so, was the evidence/source produced at the time, or many years later? (Our memories aren't always reliable.)
- Did the person have a wide perspective on the event/issue over a period of time, or was their experience of it narrow and 'localised'?

Purpose

1 Why did someone actually *bother* to create the source in the first place?
- To inform? To *mis*inform? To persuade? To make money, or some other gain?
- What sort of language is used? This might give a clue as to purpose. Emotive or strong language almost certainly communicates a particular point of view.

2 For what *audience* was the source created?
- Is it a **private document** (e.g. a diary, personal letter, etc.) that was never intended to be seen by many people? The source creator may be more honest and open in a private document (but still keep in mind the cautions in the 'Author' section above).
- Is it a **public document** (e.g. a speech, newspaper item, etc.)? In a public document the creator of the source may be influenced by what they believe their audience wants to hear, or how they might respond.

If you have an original document or object (rather than a transcript or re-creation), look at the physical nature of the source. What can you learn from its form? For example, is it an old document written on fancy paper in elegant handwriting? This might suggest that the creator was relatively wealthy and well-educated. If it was produced on scrap paper, scribbled in pencil and with spelling errors, this too will tell us something.

ISBN: 9780170418393

1 ACTIVITY

Use as many of the 'CAP' analysis questions on pages 36–37 to help you analyse the text below. The most useful questions will be from the 'Author' and 'Purpose' sections.

- Remember that you may not be able to 'answer' all of the questions, but you can speculate. (In 'real' research you would want to follow up on any speculations to test whether or not they are right.)

When finished, share your analysis with others in the class.

The following excerpt *[portion]* was taken from the book *A Child of Hitler* written by Alfons Heck in 1985. The quote tells of Heck's attendance at a speech by Adolf Hitler when Heck was a 10-year-old member of the *Jungvolk*, the 'youngsters' of the Hitler Youth. The occasion was the 1938 Nazi Party Congress, a rally held amid great pageantry *[displays]* in the ancient city of Nuremberg.

A) When Hitler finally appeared, we greeted him with a thundering triple 'Seig Heil' *['Hail the Victory']* and it took all of our discipline to end it there, as we had been instructed. Hitler, the superb actor that he was, always began his speeches quietly, almost conversationally, man to man. He then increased both tempo *[pace]* and volume steadily, but occasionally returned to the slower pace, piquing *[re-engaging]* his listeners for the next crescendo *[climax]*. It was a sure-fire method which frequently mesmerized *[captivated]* even his bitter foes or the unbelievers. We fell for it totally. I am sure none of us in that audience took our eyes off him.

B) Because of our small size, all of the youngest of the *Jungvolk* stood in the first row, about 40 feet from the podium. I don't recall the exact content of the speech 45 years later, but I'll never forget its emotional impact. In the first half-hour much of it was a surprisingly personal statement. Here was our mighty leader telling us quite humbly how hard his own adolescence *[youth]* had been, how little hope it had held and how often he had come close to utter despair, especially after the bitter defeat of Germany in World War One. He also touched on the class distinctions *[differences in wealth]* of an earlier generation, which he had now obliterated for us. And then his voice rose, took on power and became rasping with a strangely appealing intensity. It touched us physically because all of its emotions were reflected on our faces.

C) We simply became an instrument in the hands of an unsurpassed *[unequalled]* master. His right fist punctuated the air in a staccato *[burst]* of short, powerful jabs as he roared out a promise and an irresistible enticement *[offering]* because he had already proven his power to the world. 'You, my youth,' he shouted

ISBN: 9780170418393

with his eyes seemingly fixed only on me, 'are our nation's most precious guarantee for a great future, and you are destined to be the leaders of a glorious new order under the supremacy of National Socialism *[the 'Nazis']*!' He then paused and lifted both arms in a gesture of triumphant benediction *[blessing]*. 'You, my youth,' he screamed hoarsely, 'never forget that one day you will rule the world!'

D) One of my post-war professors, who himself had been a dedicated Nazi even before Hitler came to power, once explained the incredible charisma *[magnetism]* of his speeches. 'Hitler's secret was that he wasn't afraid to shout out loud what most Germans were afraid of admitting to themselves, namely that we deserved to rule the world.' Judging by our reactions to Hitler's speech, that may well be correct. We erupted into a frenzy of nationalistic pride that bordered on hysteria. For minutes on end we shouted at the top of our lungs, with tears streaming down our faces: 'Seig Heil, Seig Heil, Seig Heil!' From that moment on, I belonged to Adolf Hitler body and soul.

'CAP' analysis

1 Is this excerpt a PRIMARY or SECONDARY document? Explain your answer.

2 Overall, how reliable is this as a source? Explain your answer by pointing out the strengths and any potential weaknesses. Use your Author/Purpose analysis to inform your response.

3 What insight *[understanding]* does this source give us about Nazi Germany? In other words, in what ways would an historian find this to be USEFUL for understanding Nazi Germany? Analyse EACH of the four paragraphs.

Example: 'Large and enthusiastic crowds turned out to see/hear Hitler.' This tells us, if true, that Hitler was a popular leader in Germany, or perhaps that crowds were forced to turn up.

a ____

b ____

c ____

d ____

4 What other sorts of sources would you (as an historian) want to check to see if the views/memories of Alfons Heck were shared by others?

5 Refer to this photograph. 'We can understand the impact Hitler had on youth in particular by comparing it to the response of the crowds turning out to see Barack Obama in Dublin in 2011.' Say whether you agree or disagree with this statement. Provide an explanation and evidence for your response.

 ISBN: 9780170418393

2 ACTIVITY

Use the 'CAP' analysis questions on pages 36–37 to help you analyse the text below. The most useful questions will be from the 'Author' and 'Purpose' sections.

- Remember that you may not be able to 'answer' all of the questions, but you can speculate. (In 'real' research you would want to follow up on any speculations to test whether or not they are right.)
- When finished, share your analysis with others in the class.

WARNING: *The following content involves discussion of medical experiments on Jews during World War II. Some might find it disturbing. These experiments were conducted with the goal of improving the survival chances of German military men in a variety of situations.*

From SS-Untersturmfuhrer Rascher to his superior Reichsfuhrer-SS Himmler, 5 April 1942. (Submitted as evidence to the Trials of War Criminals before *[in front of]* the Nuremberg Military Tribunals, 1946.)

Highly esteemed *[valued]* Reich Leader:

Reich = (German) empire

Enclosed is an interim *[first draft]* report on the low-pressure experiments so far conducted in the concentration camp of Dachau … Only continuous experiments at simulated altitudes higher than 10.5km resulted in death. These experiments showed that breathing stopped after about 30 minutes, while in two cases the action of the heart continued for another 20 minutes.

The third experiment of this type took such an extraordinary course that I called an SS physician *[doctor]* of the camp as a witness, since I had worked on these experiments all by myself. It was a continuous experiment without oxygen at a height of 12km conducted on a 37-year-old Jew in good general condition. Breathing continued up to 30 minutes. After 4 minutes the experimental subject began to perspire and to wiggle his head, after 5 minutes cramps occurred, between 6 and 10 minutes breathing increased in speed and the experimental subject

Critical thinking skills

ISBN: 9780170418393

became unconscious; from 11 to 30 minutes breathing slowed down to three breaths per minute, finally stopping altogether. Severest cyanosis *[discoloration caused by lack of oxygen]* developed in between times and foam appeared at the mouth …

Autopsy [after-death] report

One hour later after breathing had stopped, the spinal cord was completely severed and the brain was removed. Thereupon the action of the auricle *[heart]* stopped for 40 seconds. It then renewed its action, coming to a complete standstill 8 minutes later. A heavy subarachnoid oedema *[bleeding]* was found in the brain. In the veins and arteries of the brain a considerable quantity of air was discovered. *[This would be a key cause of death.]*

'CAP' analysis

1 Overall, how reliable is this as a source? Explain your answer by pointing out the strengths and any potential weaknesses. Use your Author/Purpose analysis to inform your response.

2 On its own, this one source is not enough to make valid judgments about the extent of Nazi policies. What other sources would you (as a historian) want to check to see how widespread these types of experiments were?

ISBN: 9780170418393

3 ACTIVITY

Use as many of the 'CAP' analysis questions on pages 36–37 to help you analyse the text below. The most useful questions will be from the 'Author' and 'Purpose' sections.

- Remember that you may not be able to 'answer' all of the questions, but you can speculate. (In 'real' research you would want to follow up on any speculations to test whether or not they are right.)
- When finished, share your analysis with others in the class.

"FROM CAROLINA TO ALABAMA"

Mingo White, July 20th, 1858. Chester, S. Carolina.

My birth place wuz in Chester, S. Carolina. A very little uv my life wuz spent there. I wuz raised in Alabama. When I wuz er bout four er five years old, I remember thet I wuz loaded in er wagon wid er lot more people in. Whar I wuz bound I don' know. What ever become uv mymother and father I don' know until er few years ago.

One mornin' in March as I wuz told, there wuz er lot uv slave speculators there in Chester ter buy some slaves fer some Alabamaians. Well do I remember thet I wuz taken up on er stand and er lot uv people come er round and felt my muscles, arms and legs and chest, and ast(asked) me er lot uv questions. I wuz passed up by nearly all uv these men cause I wuz jest er chil Before we slaves wuz taken ter de tradin post Ole Masser Crawford, and I know all de rest uv de slave holders too, told us ter tell every body thet ast(aske) us if we'd ever been sick, to tell 'em thet we'd never been sick in our life. We had ter tell'em all sorts uv lies fer our Master or else take er beatin. We wuz scared not ter tell 'em any thang else.

I wuz jest er little thang; taken er way from my mother and father, jest when I needed 'em most. The only care thet I hador ever knowed anythang er bout wuz given ter me, a friend uv my fathers gid hit ter me.His name wuz John White. My daddy told him ter take care uv me fer him. John wuz er fiddler. Many er night I woke up ter find myself sleep twix his legs while he wuz playin fer er dance fer de white folkes. My father and mother wuz sold fro each odder too, de same time as I wuz sold. Iuse ter wonder if I had any broth brothers and sisters, as I had always wanted some.A few years later I found ou thet I didn't have any.

This is an excerpt from the life story of Mingo White, a slave on a plantation in Alabama, USA.

'CAP' analysis

Critical thinking skills

1 Overall, how reliable is this as a source? Explain your answer by pointing out the strengths and any potential weaknesses. Use your Author/Purpose analysis to inform your response.

2 On its own, this one source is not enough to make valid judgments about the nature of slave experiences. What other sources would you (as a historian) want to check to see if Mingo's story is typical of the slave experience?

 ISBN: 9780170418393

7 Historical thinking concept: Identifying continuity and change

As you will know by now, historians are not interested simply in 'what happened' in the past. Such a focus is really just a chronicle or record of events. Historians always want to explain the past in order to better understand it and to help make sense of societies and events. One of the key historical relationships they try to identify is that of continuity and/or change over time. Put simply: what things stayed the same and what things changed. The 'things' might be events, behaviours, ideas, beliefs, economic outcomes and so on. It is unusual, however, for the past to fall neatly into patterns of either continuity or change. Usually the two are intertwined and it is the historian's task to assess the evidence and decide which feature is dominant over what time frame.

Consider your own life. Clearly, your age has changed over the years so this looks like a very obvious example of 'change'. But is it that clear-cut? You could also consider your change in age as an 'ongoing process of ageing'! In this case, your life can be seen as one of 'continuity'. Which is right? Well, perhaps there is no 'right' answer to this, but it does show us how historians have to avoid jumping to premature conclusions and take the time to think hard about the processes they are analysing.

Looking at an international context, many people saw the election of Barack Obama, the USA's first black president, as representing a great change in terms of the place of blacks in American life. Others, however, point to the ongoing over-representation of blacks in negative statistics such as imprisonment, poor educational and health outcomes, drug use, and so on. To them, one black president does not make enough of an impact in the continuity of black deprivation. So, who is right? Does Obama's election represent continuity or change? Historians will debate and present arguments supported by evidence for both cases. Eventually, one view may indeed prevail *['win']*, but the key point to take from this is that engagement with the evidence and the ability to take and argue a position is more important than arriving at some supposedly 'right' answer.

1 ACTIVITY

Individual activity

On the timeline below, write in what you think have been TEN significant events in your life to date. You may use the same/similar events as you did in the activity on page 19, or different ones.

I was born

Identity any significant points of CHANGE, as well as any longer-term patterns of CONTINUITY.

Points of significant change: ______________________________

Longer-term patterns of continuity: ______________________________

 ISBN: 9780170418393

Evaluation: To what extent has your life been characterised by CHANGE? *(Circle one option and then explain your view.)*

a To a large extent

b To a moderate extent

c To a limited extent

d Very little; continuity is dominant

2 ACTIVITY

Group activity

On the timeline below, write in what you think have been TEN significant events in your group's SCHOOL life to date. You may use the same/similar events as you did in the activity on page 20, or different ones.

We started school

Identity any significant points of CHANGE, as well as any patterns of CONTINUITY.

Points of significant change: ______

Patterns of continuity: ______

Evaluation: To what extent has your group's school life been characterised by CHANGE? *(Circle one option and then explain your view.)*

a To a large extent
b To a moderate extent
c To a limited extent
d Very little; continuity is dominant

Discuss your response with other groups in the class.

ISBN: 9780170418393

Background to activities 3 and 4: 'Jim Crow' laws

Although African-American slaves were emancipated *[freed]* in 1863 during the Civil War, the southern American states where slavery had flourished were unwilling to suddenly treat blacks as equals. Despite having lost the war, southern whites were gradually able to re-establish dominance over blacks by the passing of discriminatory laws and through the use of terror by organisations such as the Ku Klux Klan. For blacks, who in some way challenged the expectations that they accept second-class status, the risks were high. At its worst, blacks could be lynched. Lynching is when a group takes the law into their own hands and kills their victim.

In 1890, an infamous court case ruled that it was legal for the southern states to separate blacks and whites, as long as they were 'separate but equal'. In a very short time this became 'separate and unequal'. The southern states began to pass a series of laws that discriminated against blacks socially, economically and politically, entrenching them as second-class citizens. These measures became known collectively as 'Jim Crow' laws. They were not fully overturned until the mid-1960s.

Note: The statistics in sources A and B (pages 50 and 51) are provided by the archives department at Tuskegee Institute *[University]*. The data do not specify victims by ethnicity or by race other than black and white. http://www.chesnuttarchive.org/classroom/lynchingstat.html

3 ACTIVITY

Refer to the maps of the United States (Source C, page 53) and the statistics in Source A (page 50) to identify any patterns of CONTINUITY and CHANGE. **Provide supporting evidence from the table.** *Remember that there is not necessarily any 'correct' answer here.* Make your case as best you can. When completed, share your views with others in the class.

Example (referring to Source B, page 51)

There appears to be *continuity* in terms of the marked drop-off in the number of lynchings from the mid-1930s. In 1936 there are eight lynchings and at no time up until the end of the period in 1968 do lynchings rise above single figures. In fact, by the early 1950s it is becoming more common to have no recorded lynchings: 11 of the 16 years (1952–68) have no recorded lynchings.

Note: You might instead consider it more valid to think about the period before and then after 1936 in terms of *change*. Your call!

Continuity: ______________________________

Critical thinking skills

Change:

Evaluation: To what extent does CHANGE describe the pattern of lynchings, by state, in the USA (Source A)? *(Circle one option and then explain your view.)*

a To a large extent
b To a moderate extent
c To a limited extent
d Very little; continuity is dominant

- Share your view with others in the class.

Source A: Lynchings, by state (1882–1968)

State	White	Black	Total
Alabama	48	299	347
Arizona	31	0	31
Arkansas	58	226	284
California	41	2	43
Colorado	65	3	68
Delaware	0	1	1
Florida	25	257	282
Georgia	39	492	531
Idaho	20	0	20
Illinois	15	19	34
Indiana	33	14	47
Iowa	17	2	19
Kansas	35	19	54
Kentucky	63	142	205
Louisiana	56	335	391
Maine	1	0	1
Maryland	2	27	29
Michigan	7	1	8
Minnesota	5	4	9
Mississippi	42	539	581
Missouri	53	69	122
Montana	82	2	84
Nebraska	52	5	57

State	White	Black	Total
Nevada	6	0	6
New Jersey	1	1	2
New Mexico	33	3	36
New York	1	1	2
North Carolina	15	86	101
North Dakota	13	3	16
Ohio	10	16	26
Oklahoma	82	40	122
Oregon	20	1	21
Pennsylvania	2	6	8
South Carolina	4	156	160
South Dakota	27	0	27
Tennessee	47	204	251
Texas	141	352	493
Utah	6	2	8
Vermont	1	0	1
Virginia	17	83	100
Washington	25	1	26
West Virginia	20	28	48
Wisconsin	6	0	6
Wyoming	30	5	35
Total	**1,297**	**3,446**	**4,743**

ISBN: 9780170418393

Source B: Lynchings, by race and year (all states combined)

Year	Whites	Blacks	Total
1882	64	49	113
1883	77	53	130
1884	160	51	211
1885	110	74	184
1886	64	74	138
1887	50	70	120
1888	68	69	137
1889	76	94	170
1890	11	85	96
1891	71	113	184
1892	69	161	230
1893	34	118	152
1894	58	134	192
1895	66	113	179
1896	45	78	123
1897	35	123	158
1898	19	101	120
1899	21	85	106
1900	9	106	115
1901	25	105	130
1902	7	85	92
1903	15	84	99
1904	7	76	83
1905	5	57	62
1906	3	62	65
1907	3	58	61
1908	8	89	97
1909	13	69	82
1910	9	67	76
1911	7	60	67
1912	2	62	64
1913	1	51	52
1914	4	51	55
1915	13	56	69
1916	4	50	54
1917	2	36	38
1918	4	60	64
1919	7	76	83
1920	8	53	61
1921	5	59	64
1922	6	51	57
1923	4	29	33
1924	0	16	16
1925	0	17	17
1926	7	23	30
1927	0	16	16
1928	1	10	11
1929	3	7	10
1930	1	20	21
1931	1	12	13
1932	2	6	8
1933	2	24	26
1934	0	15	15
1935	2	18	20
1936	0	8	8
1937	0	8	8
1938	0	6	6
1939	1	2	3
1940	1	4	5
1941	0	4	4
1942	0	6	6
1943	0	3	3
1944	0	2	2
1945	0	1	1
1946	0	6	6
1947	0	1	1
1948	1	1	2
1949	0	3	3
1950	1	1	2
1951	0	1	1
1952	0	0	0
1953	0	0	0
1954	0	0	0
1955	0	3	3
1956	0	0	0
1957	1	0	1
1958	0	0	0
1959	0	1	1
1960	0	0	0
1961	0	1	1
1962	0	0	0
1963	0	1	1
1964	2	1	3
1965	0	0	0
1966	0	0	0
1967	0	0	0
1968	0	0	0
Total	**1,297**	**3,446**	**4,743**

ISBN: 9780170418393

4 ACTIVITY

Use the maps of the United States (Source C, page 53) and the statistics in Source B (page 51) to identify any patterns of CONTINUITY and CHANGE. Provide supporting evidence from the table. *Remember that there is not necessarily any 'correct' answer here.* Make your case as best you can. When completed, share your views with others in the class.

Continuity: ______________________________

Change: ______________________________

Evaluation: To what extent does CHANGE describe the pattern of lynchings, by race and year, in the USA (Source B)? *(Circle one option and then explain your view.)*

a To a large extent
b To a moderate extent
c To a limited extent
d Very little; continuity is dominant

- Share your view with others in the class.

ISBN: 9780170418393

Source C: Maps of the United States

1861: Slave and free states

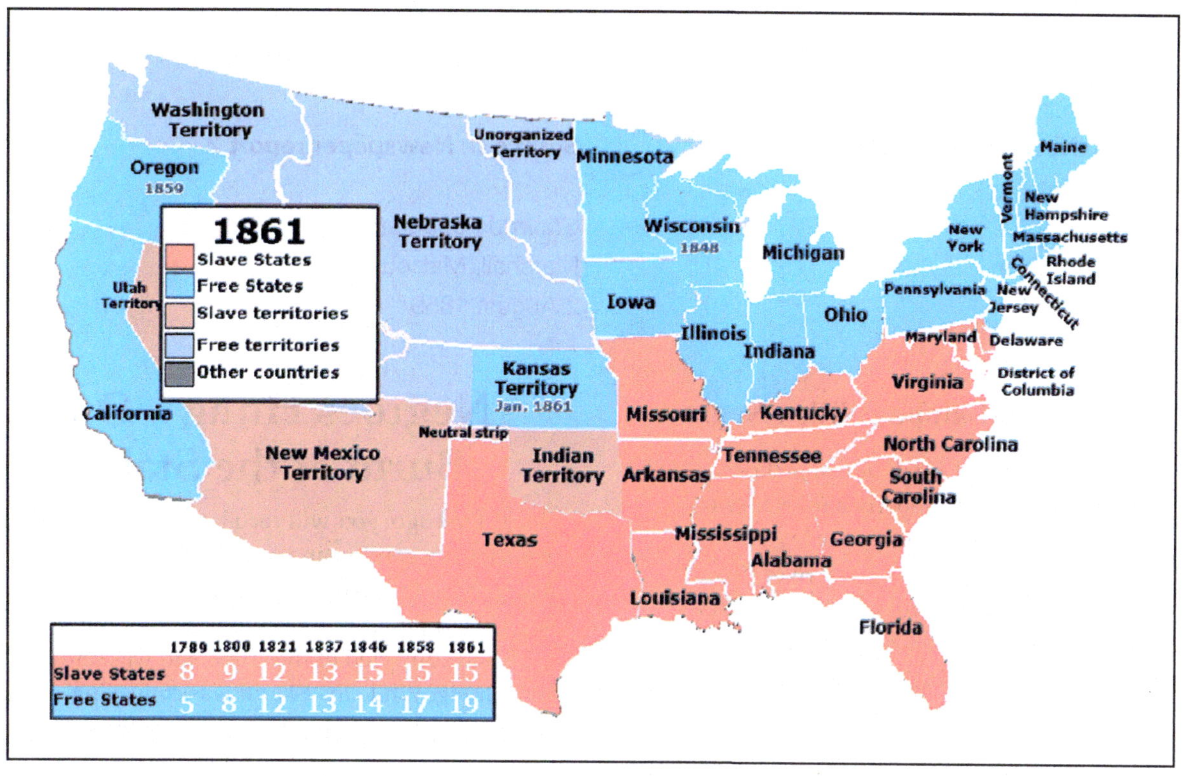

Modern map of the United States

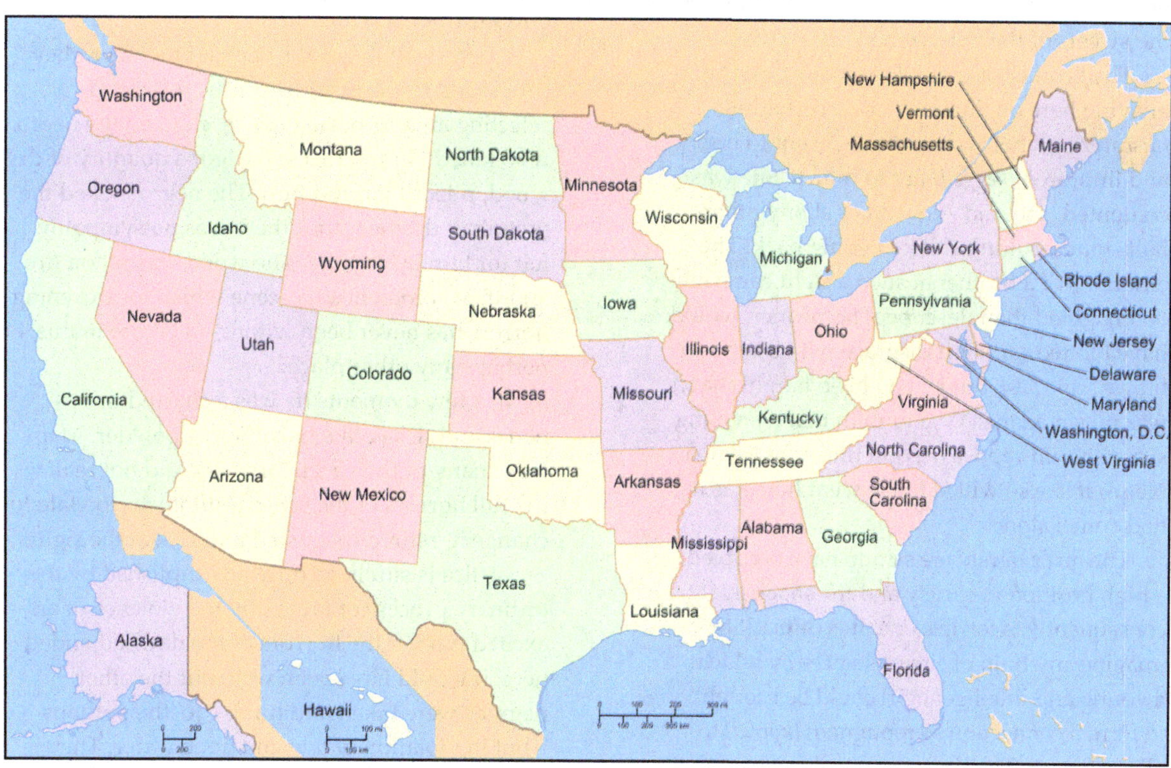

ISBN: 9780170418393

5 ACTIVITY

Both of the newspaper reports below describe events that happened in the same year but at different locations in the United States (refer to the maps of the USA, Source C, page 53).

Source D: Newspaper report 1

Valley Spirit
Windsor, Michigan
19 January 1859

A White Girl Elopes With a Negro

A young girl named Sarah Judson, whose father lives on a fine property a mile or two from Pontiac, eloped *[ran away to be married]* on Saturday and went across the river to Detroit. The partner of her flight was a black man who has been in the employment of her father for some time in the capacity of farm hand. The first that the father knew of their intention was their absence! From Detroit they immediately crossed over into Canada where was found someone who performed the marriage ceremony, and the two were made one. They are now back in Windsor, enjoying the sweets of the honeymoon.

The brother of the girl came the next day arriving here on Sunday and, ascertaining *[discovering]* their whereabouts, went to her and implored *[begged]* her to return. She was contented, she said – loved her ebony other-half – and couldn't think of going back. The emotions of a brother at such a sight can better be imagined than described. Some men would have blotted out their disgrace with a series of blows *[punches]*, but he had been taught that it was no sin against God or man that his young sister should repose *[rest]* in the embrace of a Negro if she so willed it. He went home as he had come: alone.

The girl's family are said to have occupied a high position in society and the shock is, consequently, a terrible one. It is difficult to imagine any train of circumstances by which a young and intelligent girl could be brought to form a connection so repugnant *[horrid]* to all the senses. The least we can wish is that the father may in some way be able to save his young daughter from the terrible future that now awaits her.

Source D: Newspaper report 2

Staunton Spectator
Marshall, Missouri
2 August 1859

Negroes Hung – One Burnt at the Stake*

Some time ago, you will recollect, a negro murdered a gentleman named Hinton, near Waverly, in this county. He was caught after a long search and put to jail. Yesterday he was put on trial here and convicted of the crime and was sentenced to be hung. While the Sheriff was conveying *[transferring]* him to prison he was set upon by the crowd and taken from that officer. The mob then proceeded to the jail and took from there two other negroes. One of them had attempted to kill a citizen of this place and the other had just committed an outrage upon a white girl.

After the mob got the negroes together, they proceeded to the outskirts of the town and, selecting an appropriate place, chained the negro who killed Hinton to a stake, got a quantity of dry wood, piled it around him. The negro looked the picture of despair – but there was no sympathy felt for him by anyone. The wood was set on fire and then commenced a scene which for sickening horrors has never been witnessed before in this, or perhaps any other place.

In a few moments he was a charred mass – bones and flesh alike burnt into a powder. Many, very many of the spectators, who did not realize the full horrors of the scene until it was too late to change it, retired disgusted and sick at the sight.

Justice is surely as fully accomplished by the ordinary process of law as by the violence of an excited mob. If the horrors of the day had ended here, it would have been well, but the other negroes were taken and hung – justly, perhaps – but in violation of law and good order. They exhibited no remorse.

[*Note that this is a common example of a lynching.]

ISBN: 9780170418393

Compare the newspaper reports to identify any patterns of CONTINUITY and/or CHANGE over these two different places in the USA. Provide supporting evidence from the sources. *Remember that there is not necessarily any 'correct' answer here.* Make your case as best you can. When completed, share your views with others in the class.

Continuity: ______

Change: ______

Evaluation: To what extent does CHANGE describe the attitudes towards African-Americans in these two different places in the USA? *(Circle one option and then explain your view.)*

a To a large extent
b To a moderate extent
c To a limited extent
d Very little; continuity is dominant

- Share your view with others in the class.

ISBN: 9780170418393

6 ACTIVITY

Source E: Examples of 'Jim Crow' laws in the southern United States

If needed, refer to the 'Background' text, top of page 49.

1 Study the different state laws below, all in effect in the southern states over the same period (1920s).

2 Identify any **CONTINUITY** (across or within states) evident in these various laws. Consider this in terms of types of behaviour/activities/situations they are prohibiting or regulating. (In a democracy, the laws that are passed tell us about the beliefs of the lawmakers and, by extension, of the people who elect them.)

- Make notes in the column 'Intent of the laws', then summarise your findings at the end.
- When completed, share your views with others in the class.

It shall be unlawful to conduct a restaurant or other place for the serving of food in the city, at which white and colored people are served in the same room, unless such white and colored persons are effectually separated by a solid partition extending from the floor upward to a distance of seven feet or higher, and unless a separate entrance from the street is provided for each compartment. **Alabama**

Every employer of white or negro males shall provide for such white or negro males reasonably accessible and separate toilet facilities. **Alabama**

The marriage of a person of Caucasian blood with a Negro, Mongolian, Malay, or Hindu shall be null and void *[cancelled]*. **Arizona**

All marriages between a white person and a negro, or between a white person and a person of negro descent to the fourth generation inclusive, are hereby forever prohibited. **Florida**

Any negro man and white woman, or any white man and negro woman, who are not married to each other, who shall habitually *[regularly]* live in and occupy in the night-time the same room shall each be punished by imprisonment not exceeding twelve (12) months, or by fine not exceeding five hundred dollars ($500.00). **Florida**

It shall be unlawful for a white person to marry anyone except a white person. Any marriage in violation of this section shall be void. **Georgia**

The officer in charge shall not bury, or allow to be buried, any colored persons upon ground set apart or used for the burial of white persons. **Georgia**

Intent of the laws

 ISBN: 9780170418393

All persons licensed to conduct a restaurant, shall serve either white people exclusively or colored people exclusively and shall not sell to the two races within the same room or serve the two races anywhere under the same license. **Georgia**

Any person … who shall rent any part of any such building to a negro person or a negro family when such building is already in whole or in part in occupancy by a white person or white family, or vice versa when the building is in occupancy by a negro person or negro family, shall be guilty of a crime and shall be punished by a fine of not less than twenty-five dollars ($25.00) nor more than one hundred dollars ($100.00) or be imprisoned not less than 10, or more than 60 days, or both such fine and imprisonment in the discretion *[choice]* of the court. **Louisiana**

The board of trustees shall … maintain a separate building … on separate ground for the admission, care, instruction, and support of all blind persons of the colored or black race. **Louisiana**

All marriages between a white person and a negro, or between a white person and a person of negro descent, to the third generation, inclusive, or between a white person and a member of the Malay race; or between the negro and a member of the Malay race; or between a person of Negro descent, to the third generation, inclusive, and a member of the Malay race, are forever prohibited, and shall be void. **Maryland**

Railroads. All railroad companies and corporations, and all persons running or operating cars or coaches by steam on any railroad line or track in the State of Maryland, for the transportation of passengers, are hereby required to provide separate cars or coaches for the travel and transportation of the white and colored passengers. **Maryland**

Separate schools shall be maintained for the children of the white and colored races. **Mississippi**

The marriage of a white person with a negro or mulatto *[mixed race]* or person who shall have one-eighth or more of negro blood, shall be unlawful and void. **Mississippi**

Intent of the laws

ISBN: 9780170418393

Any instructor who shall teach in any school, college or institution where members of the white and colored race are received and enrolled as pupils for instruction shall be deemed guilty of a misdemeanor *[wrong-doing]*, and upon conviction thereof, shall be fined in any sum not less than ten dollars ($10.00) nor more than fifty dollars ($50.00) for each offense. **Oklahoma**

The Conservation Commission shall have the right to make segregation of the white and colored races as to the exercise of rights of fishing, boating and bathing. **Oklahoma**

No persons, firms, or corporations, which furnish *[provide]* meals to passengers at station restaurants or station eating houses, in times limited by common carriers of said passengers, shall furnish said meals to white and colored passengers in the same room, or at the same table, or at the same counter. **South Carolina**

Child Custody. It shall be unlawful for any parent, relative, or other white person in this State, having the control or custody of any white child, by right of guardianship, natural or acquired, or otherwise, to dispose of, give or surrender such white child permanently into the custody, control, maintenance, or support, of a negro. **South Carolina**

Intent of the laws

ISBN: 9780170418393

7 ACTIVITY

Summarise your notes on the various state laws to identify any patterns of **CONTINUITY** over these different places, in terms of types of behaviour/activities/situations that are being prohibited or regulated. Provide supporting evidence from the sources. *Remember that there is not necessarily any 'correct' answer here.* Make your case as best you can. When completed, share your views with others in the class.

Continuity: ____

8 ACTIVITY

Refer to the information in either or both sources F and G (pages 59 and 60). Identify any patterns of CONTINUITY and/or CHANGE over time. Provide supporting evidence from the sources. *Remember that there is not necessarily any 'correct' answer here.* Make your case as best you can. When completed, share your views with others in the class.

Source F: Race relations in USA: Intermarriage

		Interracial married couples					
		Black/white			Other		
Year	**Total married couples**	**Total Black/ White**	**Black husband, white wife**	**White husband, black wife**	**White/ Other race***	**Black/ Other race***	**Total all interracial married couples**
1960	40,491,000	51,000	25,000	26,000	90,000	7,000	148,000
1970	44,598,000	65,000	41,000	24,000	233,000	12,000	310,000
1980	49,514,000	121,000	94,000	27,000	785,000	47,000	953,000
1990	51,718,000	213,000	159,000	54,000	1,173,000	75,000	1,461,000
1995	54,937,000	328,000	206,000	122,000	988,000	76,000	1,392,000

* includes mainly Asian, Hispanic and American Indians.

Source: Pew Research

Critical thinking skills

ISBN: 9780170418393

Source G: Historical public opinion of approval/disapproval of interracial marriage in the United States

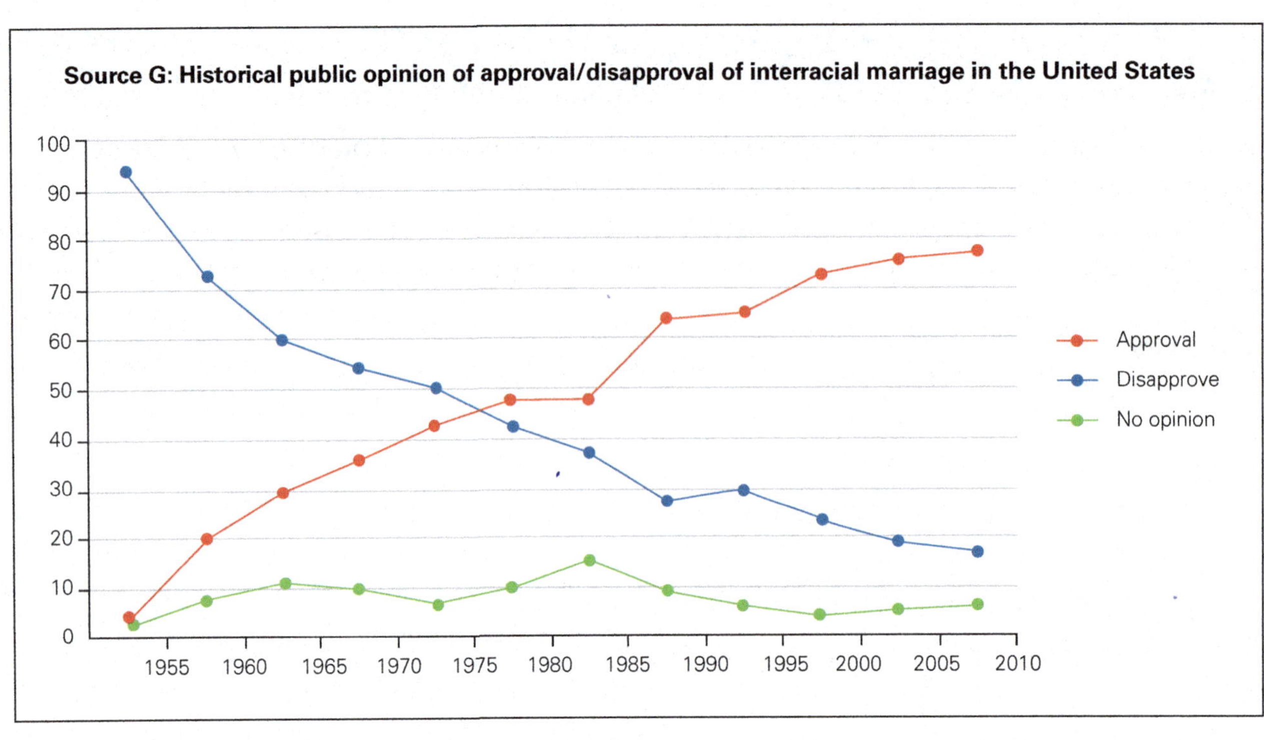

Continuity:

Change:

ISBN: 9780170418393

Evaluation: To what extent does CHANGE describe interracial marriage in the USA? *(Circle one option and then explain your view.)*

a To a large extent
b To a moderate extent
c To a limited extent
d Very little; continuity is dominant

- Share your view with others in the class.

9 ACTIVITY

Final evaluation

Use evidence from any/all of Sources A–G to evaluate the extent to which, in your view, CONTINUITY or CHANGE describes race relations in the USA over time and/or place. Provide evidence to support your response.

- Share your view with others in the class.

8 Historical thinking concept: Analysing cause and consequence

Causes

In their study of events in the past, historians are always interested in the questions of **how** and **why**; in other words, what were the *causes* of the events being studied. There are usually the more obvious short-term causes, those things that act like a spark. However, it is often the long-term and underlying causes of events that interest historians more, and get them debating more. As Seixas and Morton say: 'Causes are multiple and layered, involving both long-term ideologies, institutions, and conditions, and short-term motivations, actions and events. Causes that are offered for any particular event (and the priority of various causes) may differ, based on the scale of the history and the approaches of the historian.' We should thus always be suspicious of simplistic explanations, the sort that unscrupulous politicians like.

Right now you are sitting in a classroom, or perhaps somewhere else, reading this. Clearly, there are a series of immediate events that have got you to this point. Maybe you came to school, attended class, had this workbook with you, then followed the teacher's instructions and opened it to this page. These are all short-term causes of you starting this activity and, as you can imagine, there could be a great many of them. There is also a range of possible long-term causes: perhaps you enjoyed History last year and did well in it so decided to take it again this year. If so, that is quite a critical decision that you made some time ago that led directly to you being here. There are also some other factors that are less direct but also played their part.

Environmental factors

Historians are mostly interested in events that involve people in the causes and consequences; however, sometimes the causes especially can include non-human factors, such as environmental changes. For example, in the late fourth century the Huns were the first of a series of invaders into Europe from the east. Based on climate evidence, it is believed that three 'mega-droughts' struck Central Asia between AD 360 and 550, the first of which was the worst drought in the history of the region in the last 2000 years. With food supplies threatened, the Huns expanded westwards in search of more fertile lands, driving deep into the eastern territories of the Roman Empire. This added even more pressure to the political and economic problems that would eventually see the decline and end of the Western Roman Empire.

ISBN: 9780170418393

For example, it is a legal requirement in New Zealand that young people attend school, at least until the age of 16. This might be considered an underlying cause of you sitting where you are now, a deeper factor that did not directly lead to you reading this text but is important nonetheless. At some point, though, the historian will decide that many possible underlying or long-term causes are just too remote to have made any meaningful contribution. For example, while 'being born' is a (very) long-term cause of you reading this today, realistically the link is very tenuous *[weak]*.

As you can imagine, historians will not always agree on where the line should be drawn between short-term, long-term and underlying causes. They also might differ on which possible causes of an event are significant enough to have had a real impact. Once more though, it is engagement with the ideas and the presentation of evidence to support an argument that helps deepen our understanding of the past events we study.

Immediate or trigger causes

Sometimes you might see short-term causes broken down further. A common additional 'category' of cause is 'immediate' or 'trigger'. As the names suggest, there is not much of a gap in time between an 'immediate' or 'trigger' cause and the event itself. Here's an example:

In 1992 in Los Angeles a series of riots broke out that lasted almost a week. In total, 58 people were killed, more than 2000 people were injured and more than 11,000 were arrested. The damage to buildings and other property was estimated at over US$1 billion. The key underlying cause was racial tension based on long-standing inequality, poverty and discrimination. Long-term causes included a history of police targeting African-Americans and treating them violently. A short-term cause was the excessively violent arrest on 3 March of Rodney King, captured on video tape. The immediate or trigger cause came on 29 April after a trial jury acquitted *[declared innocent]* the four accused officers of the Los Angeles Police Department. Peaceful protests began within half an hour, but these soon escalated into a full-scale riot.

1 ACTIVITY

Causes

Consider the causes of you being where you are right now and doing what you are doing right now.

1 Under the heading 'Draft notes: trigger causes', note down two or three of what you consider to be the most important trigger/immediate causes.
2 Do the same for 'short-term causes'.
3 Do the same for 'long-term causes'.
4 And finally, the 'underlying causes'.
5 Write your final choices onto the timeline.

Note: Your first task really will be to decide where you 'draw the line' between 'trigger/immediate', 'short-term', 'long-term' and 'underlying' causes.

The present

Draft notes: 'Trigger' causes

Draft notes: Short-term causes

Draft notes: Long-term causes

Draft notes: Underlying causes

 ISBN: 9780170418393

2 ACTIVITY

Reflection

1 Where did you decide to 'draw the line' between what you considered to be trigger/immediate, short-term, long-term and underlying causes? What criteria did you use to help make the decision?

2 Explain your **reasons** for including what you consider to be the most significant causes for each of the following:

- Immediate/trigger
- Short-term
- Long-term
- Underlying

ISBN: 9780170418393

Analysing sources to detect 'causes'

To help you decide what might be trigger/immediate and short-term, long-term or underlying causes, the sort of words below (and others like them) might alert you to these relationships. You could also use these words yourself when writing about causes of events.

Causes	Possible words to look for in a text (or use in a written response)
Trigger/immediate and/or short-term	directly, instantly, abruptly, initiated, prompted, incited, kindled, sparked
Long-term and/or underlying	led to, contributed to, made possible, increasing, growing, resulted in, encouraged, inspired, blocked, prevented

3 ACTIVITY

As you read how Britain arrived at the decision to present Maori with the Treaty of Waitangi, try to identify (highlight/annotate) all of the main causes. *Note that in the interests of keeping this manageable, we will not look at any possible trigger/immediate causes. Consider each of the following:*

- Short-term
- Long-term
- Underlying

Tip: You'll need to, at some point, decide where you draw the line between each of these categories – you decide!

When you are satisfied with your findings, write them into the table on page 69 in brief bullet point form. *Remember that it is unlikely that everyone will agree on what goes where. Make your own decisions but have a reason for them.*

Why Britain offered Maori a Treaty in 1840

In 1840 Britain sought a Treaty with as many Maori as would sign, despite its earlier reluctance to become involved in another colony because of all the problems that this could bring. Britain at this time preferred a good trading relationship from which it could get the resources it wanted without any formal ties. However, a series of events and developments led Britain to believe that it had to intervene.

1) Historian Peter Adams states that the growing lawlessness of British people already in New Zealand worried Britain so much that it felt it must negotiate with Maori for authority to govern them. The problem was not a new one. Serious concerns had been raised in 1830 by the *Elizabeth* incident in particular. This began when a Captain Stewart transported Te Rauparaha's warriors to Akaroa in the South Island, where they decimated *[destroyed]* the local Ngai Tahu hapu. This caused great alarm in Britain because Pakeha had become directly involved in inter-hapu rivalries; Britain feared that such behaviour could escalate and lead to further massacres. Meanwhile, in the Bay of Islands Christian missionaries – who

Annotations

 ISBN: 9780170418393

had been in New Zealand working among Maori since 1815 – encouraged a number of chiefs in 1831 to call on the British government to do something about Pakeha troublemakers in the north. A British official, James Busby, arrived in 1833 but he had been given no means to enforce his authority, meaning no improvement in the situation.

2) Adding to the pressure on Britain to act was another pressing matter. The New Zealand Company had been established in London in 1838 with the goal of purchasing vast areas of land cheaply from Maori in order to establish large numbers of migrants in the new settlements they planned to create. British officials worried that if lawlessness was a problem with about 2000 Pakeha in New Zealand, it would be far worse with 10,000 or more. Furthermore, Britain was also concerned that these new settlements might set themselves up as republics – self-governing independent towns not bound by British law. In late 1839 the Company's first ship, the *Tory*, had arrived to begin these purchases; Britain felt that it would have to act quickly.

3) As if that wasn't enough, the historian James Belich points out that investors were also pressuring Britain to act, worried that lawlessness would threaten their profits. British and Sydney capitalists had sunk substantial amounts of money into New Zealand since the 1810s. This included the many whaling stations around the coast, as well as timber mills and the Horeke shipyard in the Hokianga (Northland), totalling an estimated £700,000. Profits were good. In the 1830s, exports from New Zealand had more than doubled and annual shipping in the Bay of Islands had increased from 89 ships in 1833 to 155 in 1839. Because lawlessness threatened such profits, investors used their considerable influence to further urge the British government to act.

4) In addition to the events leading up to 1840 there was a belief among Britain's leaders that it was Britain's destiny (and, indeed, duty) to spread its 'civilised' ways throughout the 'unenlightened' world – a noble mission. (This idea of the 'White Man's Burden' would be put into poetic form in1899 by the pro-Empire Rudyard Kipling.) Many within the British government felt that taking control in New Zealand was almost an inevitable *[inescapable]* consequence of the earlier arrival of British sealers, whalers and traders. They in turn had been attracted there by Captain Cook's reports of plentiful resources, published after his late 18th-century voyages of exploration – which literally put New Zealand on the world

Critical thinking skills

ISBN: 9780170418393

map. Belief in British superiority had been developing for some centuries as its ships and sailors had explored new lands around the globe.

5) British humanitarian organisations also exerted influence in the British parliament to ensure that Maori would not be exploited by Europeans. Two key organisations were the Aborigines Protection Society (APS) and Church Missionary Society (CMS). They were determined that Maori society would not be damaged in the same way that Aborigines and Native Americans had since colonisation began there in the 18th and 17th centuries respectively. The timing was good, for the 1830s marked the high point of the influence of these humanitarian groups – they had already successfully campaigned for the abolition of the slave trade throughout the British Empire in 1833. Sir James Stephen, perhaps the most powerful unelected official in the British Empire, was a deeply religious member of the Church Missionary Society. His 'boss' at the time the Treaty was first being considered, Secretary of State for the Colonies Lord Glenelg, was too. Between them these two men were most responsible for recommending that Britain step into New Zealand.

6) A final factor, if not as immediate as the others, was a niggling concern in Britain that France and perhaps even the USA might be interested in New Zealand. The sole British official stationed in New Zealand, the frustrated and self-important James Busby, sent back alarmist reports about the Frenchman Baron Charles de Thierry and his (wild) claim in 1837 of setting himself up as King of New Zealand from a base in the Hokianga. The British government did not take Busby seriously, but there was a general concern that its rival of many centuries, France, was increasing its influence in the area. There was already a French Catholic bishop (Pompallier) at Kororareka (modern-day Russell). Britain was also aware that a French company's immigrant ship was already on its way to Akaroa in the South Island. It was unclear whether this might be the beginning of a flood of French migrants. In addition, an American consul resided on the Hokianga harbour. He was thought to be warning Maori off any formal relationship with Britain.

ISBN: 9780170418393

Summary of causes		
Short-term	**Long-term**	**Underlying**

1 Explain why you 'drew the line' between your different causes where you did:

- between short-term and long-term: ______________________

- between long-term and underlying: ______________________

2 Prioritising causes. Using only the text above, which one or two causes do YOU think were the most significant in terms of convincing Britain to offer Maori a Treaty? Give your reasons.

- Share your view with others in the class.

4 ACTIVITY

As you read why many Maori finally decided to sign the Treaty of Waitangi document, try to identify (highlight/annotate) all of the main causes. *Note that in the interests of keeping this manageable, we will not look at any possible trigger/immediate causes. Consider each of the following:*

- Short-term
- Long-term
- Underlying

Tip: You'll need to, at some point, decide where you draw the line between each of these categories – you decide!

When you are satisfied with your findings, write them into the table below in brief bullet point form. *Remember that it is unlikely that everyone will agree on what goes where. Make your own decisions but have a reason for them.*

Why many Maori chiefs signed the Treaty

In 1840 many (but not all) Maori from Northland and beyond accepted a Treaty with Britain, despite expressing many reservations about the need for one. Signing the Treaty formalised the relationship between Britain and those Maori chiefs who signed. William Hobson was Britain's representative who presented Maori with the Treaty; he became New Zealand's first governor once it was signed.

1) Historian Peter Adams points out that Maori, as well as Christian missionaries and the British Resident James Busby, were concerned about Pakeha lawlessness and the increase in disregard for Maori ways. Encouraged by missionaries, in 1831 northern chiefs had called on the British to do something about the trouble-makers. James Busby had arrived in 1833, but he had been given no means to enforce his authority. Maori thus called him a 'Man o' War *[warship]* without guns'. In light of this failure of British authority, Maori could not be sure what problems unregulated Pakeha settlement might bring in the future, so some thought it was better to agree to the British intervening to look after their own people.

2) Maori had already demonstrated an enthusiasm for European ways in the preceding decades, so were receptive to the idea of a closer bond. Maori such as Moehanga in 1809 and Hongi Hika in 1820 (both Nga Puhi) were among those who had visited England and liked what they saw there; they had encouraged their people to continue the positive relationship. The tribes most in contact with Pakeha were thus keen to continue trading and to also regulate it where difficulties were occurring. These difficulties included the growing arrogance and disrespect of the Pakeha as their numbers increased. Something needed to be done and a Treaty might well be the answer.

Annotations

ISBN: 9780170418393

3) In addition to a desire for trade, the links between Maori and the outside world were longest and strongest with Britain. Maori traditions held that the British were the first to make contact with the Maori people, from the time of Cook's first visit in 1769 and his subsequent countrywide explorations. Thereafter, British nationals living in New Zealand outnumbered those from other countries – there were roughly 2000 Europeans by 1840, all of them British apart from about 50 Americans and 20 French. English missionaries such as Henry Williams were also a trusted contact point between Britain and Maori. Furthermore, the relationship with British governors in Australia had begun as early as 1804 when the Nga Puhi chief Te Pahi sent his son to Sydney. While there he was looked after by the governor of New South Wales, Philip Gidley King. Many more Maori crossed the Tasman and were hosted by a succession of governors: the relationship was close and positive.

4) In counterpoint to this, rumours that other less desirable powers were showing an interest in New Zealand concerned some Maori. Historian Peter Tremewen points out that northern Maori had concerns about the French in particular. In 1772, Bay of Islands Maori had killed the French captain Marion du Fresne and two dozen of his men; after five weeks of peaceful relations, du Fresne had finally worn out his welcome. In line with Maori beliefs and customs, they fully expected French utu *['pay-back']* at some point. Maori were also aware of the harsh French treatment of the Tahitians. (Maori were less sympathetic to the Aborigines, who they viewed as inferior.) Maori were also aware of Britain's victory over Napoleon's French armies in 1815. Historian Claudia Orange notes that the chief Titore, 'acknowledging Britain's past conflict with France, offered to reserve certain trees from which spars *[for ship masts]* could be cut in any future Anglo-French engagement.'

5) In terms of the Treaty itself, the personal and almost sacred nature of the relationship between Maori and the Queen was emphasised. Both James Busby and William Hobson took this line, but it was the assurances of the Christian missionaries that really convinced Maori. As historian Claudia Orange points out: 'On his seven visits to New Zealand between 1814 and 1839, he [missionary Samuel Marsden] consistently promoted the belief that the Crown had a parental interest in protecting the Maori people ... Maori came to expect a personal relationship with the Crown's representative ...'. Maori were allowed to believe during the discussions in February 1840 that any problems that might arise in the future

Critical thinking skills

ISBN: 9780170418393

could be worked out directly with the Queen if required. In addition, there was a guarantee to protect Maori from Pakeha trouble-makers, convincing most Maori that the Treaty would be honoured.

6) In addition to the assurance of a covenant *[solemn bond]* between chiefs and the Queen, in the Maori version of the Treaty, rangatiratanga (chiefly authority) was guaranteed. The neologism *[new word]* 'kawanatanga' was used to incorrectly translate the English word 'sovereignty', thus for Maori there was no apparent loss of their chiefly authority. As Nopera Panakaeroa of the Rarawa tribe said: 'Only the shadow of the land passes to the Queen. The substance stays with us.' Furthermore, an official Pakeha presence did not appear threatening, as the country was without a doubt a Maori one. Maori were culturally, militarily, politically, numerically and economically dominant. There were only about 2000 Pakeha while there were some 90,000 Maori. Furthermore, they were battle-hardened after fighting each other in the Musket Wars of the 1820s and 1830s, so could certainly hold their own militarily.

7) Finally, historian Manuka Henare notes that powerful traditional inter-hapu rivalries were being played out in the discussions around the Treaty. Some hapu, particularly northern ones, hoped to take advantage of the benefits it was believed the formal presence of the British government would bring. Other tribes further south were determined not to let Nga Puhi monopolise *[control]* the relationship with the British Crown, as they had done with iron, muskets, missionaries and literacy in the previous decades. Hone Heke of Nga Puhi was equally determined that he would be the one to manipulate the relationship in his tribe's favour. Thus the age-old 'pursuit of mana' also played its part in convincing various Maori chiefs to sign.

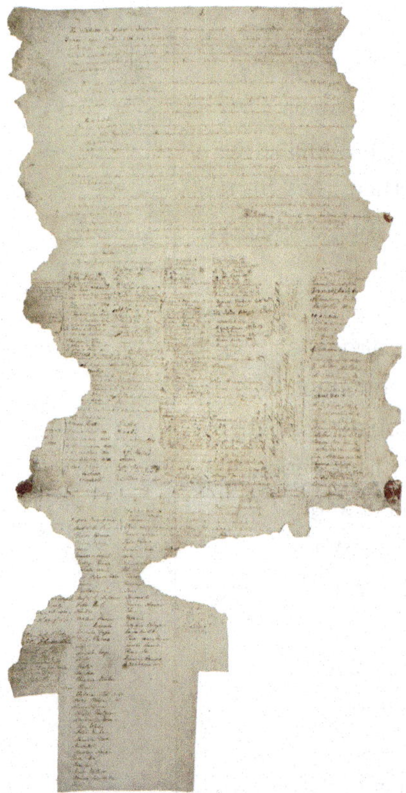

ISBN: 9780170418393

Summary of causes		
Short-term	**Long-term**	**Underlying**

1 Explain why you 'drew the line' between your different causes where you did:

- between short-term and long-term: ______________________________

- between long-term and underlying: ______________________________

2 Prioritising causes. Using only the text above, which one or two causes do you think were the most significant in terms of convincing many Maori to sign the Treaty? Give your reasons.

- Share your view with others in the class.

ISBN: 9780170418393

'PEST' analysis of causes

Considering the causes of historical events in terms of trigger, short-term, long-term and underlying factors is not the only way to think about them. In fact, the more ways we think about causes (and consequences) the deeper our understanding of the past grows.

The so-called 'PEST' analysis involves examining the causes of historical events in terms of political, economic, social and technological factors. To this we could add military, environmental (see page 62) and cultural factors as valid ways to think about causes, but it seems that 'PESTMEC' has not yet become a popular mnemonic *[memory aid]*. As always with History, there is not necessarily any clear line between these various factors and most - if not all – of the causes could be categorised in more than one. However, there are some general guidelines to help you decide where a particular causal factor might best fit.

Political: this is to do with power in a society, but is not focused solely on political leaders. For example, feminists argue that gender politics in society significantly affects how women are treated, irrespective of what the law might say. 'Politics' can describe the power relationships between individuals, groups and countries and can involve the use of law, military might, or just social customs and expectations.

Economic: this generally involves the generation, control and distribution of wealth (both money and goods). Economic factors often overlap with political (wealth is power) and social (who has wealth and who does not).

Social: this factor is often seen as part of the 'history from below' approach. Its focus is on the people rather than political or economic leaders. It considers the cultural groups that people identify with and how those groups interact with each other. 'Culture' is a broad term that includes ethnicity, wealth, sexuality, gender, political beliefs and so on.

Technological: technology can be defined as 'the tools and machines that may be used to solve real-world problems'; those tools include everything from a safety pin to a satellite. Historians are interested in how technology has affected societies, from the nature of work, to health issues, to the layout of cities.

5 ACTIVITY

Refer to 'Why Britain offered Maori a Treaty in 1840', pages 66–68.

- Read each paragraph and decide which **one** of the 'PEST' causal factors the paragraph **best** describes. (You may well find that there are other categories that would work as well – good! However, for the purposes of this activity identify what you think is the main one.)
- Once you have decided upon the best 'PEST' factor, write the paragraph number and a brief description of the factor into the appropriate box below. *The first paragraph has been done for you as an example.*

ISBN: 9780170418393

Political	Economic
Paragraph 1: dealing with the growing Pakeha lawlessness.	
Social	**Technological**

6 ACTIVITY

Refer to 'Why many Maori chiefs signed the Treaty', pages 70–72, and carry out the same process from Activity 5.

Political	Economic
Social	**Technological**

ISBN: 9780170418393

Agency versus structure

Another way to consider the causes and events is to think in terms of 'agency' and 'structure'. Sociologist Chris Barker, in *Cultural Studies: Theory and Practice*, describes '**agency**' as 'the capacity *[ability]* of individuals or groups to act independently and to make their own free choices. By contrast, '**structure**' is those factors of influence (such as social class, religion, gender, ethnicity, ability, customs, etc.) that determine or limit a person and the decisions that they can realistically make.' In other words, 'agency' is where a person or group mostly control the decisions they make, while 'structural' factors tend to limit or act against freedom of action.

This leads us to consider the extent to which an individual or group has influenced events, as opposed to just having been swept along more or less helplessly. For example, slaves in Brazil in the 18th century had limited agency because under the structure of slavery, their owners controlled most (but not all) of the decisions that they could make. In addition to this, the legal, social, political and economic systems of the ruling class all supported the institution of slavery.

Here is another, different, situation: some people argue that social structures in today's society still limit women's agency. For example, when men speak on behalf of women, this denies them agency. Being dismissive of women's work or lowering its value simply because it is done by women is another example; so is having fictional female characters to are always secondary to men.

So, do historians all agree on where the line between 'structure' and 'agency' lies in any given historical setting? Of course not! Once again, it is the tussle of ideas and evidence that deepens our understanding of the past.

7 ACTIVITY

Refer to the appropriate paragraph in the text (pages 66–68) as noted. Decide where you will position yourself, from **1** to **4**, for each of the following statements (there are no 'half' positions). Provide a brief explanation of your choice. When finished, discuss your responses with the rest of the class.

1 = strongly agree
2 = agree
3 = disagree
4 = strongly disagree

Circle the appropriate number below for each statement.

ISBN: 9780170418393

Text: Why Britain offered Maori a Treaty in 1840

The British government did not really have agency in dealing with pressure from ...

... **Pakeha lawlessness**. (Paragraph 1)

Your position: 1 2 3 4

Explanation: ______

... **the New Zealand Company**. (Paragraph 2)

Your position: 1 2 3 4

Explanation: ______

... **investors**. (Paragraph 3)

Your position: 1 2 3 4

Explanation: ______

... **the 'White Man's Burden'**. (Paragraph 4)

Your position: 1 2 3 4

Explanation: ______

... **the (British) Humanitarian Movement**. (Paragraph 5)

Your position: 1 2 3 4

Explanation: ______

... **concerns about the French**. (Paragraph 6)

Your position: 1 2 3 4

Explanation: ______

Critical thinking skills

Overall view

Britain did not really have agency when it came to the decision to present Maori with the Treaty of Waitangi.

Your position: 1 2 3 4

Explanation: ______

8 ACTIVITY

Refer to the appropriate paragraph in the text (pages 70–72) as noted. Decide where you will position yourself, from **1** to **4**, for each of the following statements (there are no 'half' positions). Provide a brief explanation of your choice. When finished, discuss your responses with the rest of the class.

1 = strongly agree
2 = agree
3 = disagree
4 = strongly disagree

Circle the appropriate number below for each statement.

Text: Why many Maori chiefs signed the Treaty

Maori chiefs did not really have agency when it came to ...

... Pakeha lawlessness. (Paragraph 1)

Your position: 1 2 3 4

Explanation: ______

... their desire for trade. (Paragraph 2)

Your position: 1 2 3 4

Explanation: ______

... choosing whether or not to continue their relationship with Britain. (Paragraph 3)

Your position: 1 2 3 4

Explanation: ______

 ISBN: 9780170418393

... accepting a relationship with Britain in order to gain protection from France. (Paragraph 4)

Your position: 1 2 3 4

Explanation: ______________________________

____

____

... accepting the guarantees said to be in the Treaty. (Paragraphs 5 and 6)

Your position: 1 2 3 4

Explanation: ______________________________

____

____

... overcoming inter-hapu rivalries. (Paragraph 7)

Your position: 1 2 3 4

Explanation: ______________________________

____

____

Overall view

Maori did not really have agency when it came to the decision to sign the Treaty of Waitangi.

Your position: 1 2 3 4

Explanation: ______________________________

____

____

____

____

Summary

When you do your planning for a causes/consequences essay or when you approach a source, try to think about the causes of an event in terms of what has been covered here:

- short-term (and perhaps 'trigger' or 'immediate' causes)
- long-term
- underlying
- PEST: political, economic, social, technological (also military, environmental, etc.)
- agency (or not)
- prioritising in terms of significance.

Remember that taking a thoughtful position and arguing it persuasively, backed by evidence, is what historians do. Don't get tied up too much in thinking that there is a single 'right' answer.

Consequences

The events historians are interested in are those that have significant consequences, such as social, economic, political, environmental, technological and so on. *See also the section on 'significance', page 21.* Usually these consequences can be usefully separated into 'short-term' (and perhaps immediate) and 'long-term'. There will, of course, not necessarily be agreement on what these are, or where to draw the line between them.

9 ACTIVITY

Consider the consequences of you being where you are right now and doing what you are doing right now.

1 Under the heading 'Draft notes: immediate consequences', note down two or three of what you consider to be the most important of these.
2 Do the same for 'short-term consequences'.
3 Do the same for 'long-term consequences'.
4 Write your final choices onto the timeline.

Note: Your first task really will be to decide where you 'draw the line' between 'immediate', 'short-term', and 'long-term' and 'underlying' consequences.

Reflection

Where did you decide to 'draw the line' between what you considered to be short-term and long-term consequences? What criteria did you use to help make the decision?

____

____

____

The present

Draft notes: immediate consequences

Draft notes: short-term consequences

Draft notes: long-term consequences

 ISBN: 9780170418393

Analysing sources to detect 'consequences'

To help you decide what might be immediate, short-term and long-term consequences, the words below (and others like them) might alert you to these relationships. You could also use these words yourself when writing about consequences of events.

Historians are very interested in how the causes of events – the political, social, economic, military forces shaping how people behave and what they desire – can be linked to the consequences of any actions they take. In any assessed work on causes and consequences, you should make the link clear.

Consequences	Possible words to look for in a text
Immediate and/or short-term	resulted, effects, outcome, corollary, aftermath, repercussion, impact, upshot, ramification, at first
Long-term	lasting/long-lasting, permanent, lifelong, enduring, ongoing, irreversible, continuing, persisting,
Links between causes and consequences	made worse, exacerbated, quickened, accelerated, strengthened, reinforced, underpinned, increased, weakened, blocked, reduced. *Note: All of these words suggest that there has been some change from 'before' to 'after'.*

Consequences of signing the Treaty of Waitangi, up to 1900

Both the British Crown and Maori went into the Treaty with certain expectations of what it would bring. Unfortunately, differences in the translation from English to Maori of some key words meant that the expectations of the two sides were not identical. This would create problems in the long-term. The consequences in the text below are set out in terms of political, military, economic and cultural impacts. This is not the only way that the consequences could be thought about.

Critical thinking skills

10 ACTIVITY

Read through the text and then, as best you can and using your own judgment, re-categorise the main points into **short-term** and **long-term consequences** of the signing of the Treaty.

- Highlight and annotate on the text to guide your thinking, then write your findings into the chart on page 85 in bullet point form.
  ***Note**: As you read through and become more familiar with the consequences, you will need to decide where you will 'draw the line' between short-term and long-term. Remember that we are only considering up to 1900.*
- **When finished, discuss your responses with the rest of the class.**

Although we commemorate 6 February as the day the Treaty was signed, it in fact took another four months to gain enough chiefs' signatures from around the country for William Hobson to feel that he could declare British sovereignty over New Zealand. He did this on 21 May 1840; he was finally formally confirmed as Governor of New Zealand in May 1841, although he had in reality been fulfilling this role since his arrival.

ISBN: 9780170418393

1) **Politically**, after the signing of the Treaty the British Crown believed itself to be the sole governing authority, although power soon shifted from the governor to a settler parliament. William Hobson died in 1842 and was replaced by Robert FitzRoy, who in turn was replaced in 1845 by George Grey, the most influential of all the governors. The reality was, though, that while the settlers immediately came under British authority, the governors at first could do very little without the compliance *[agreement]* of Maori, who were still dominant in all meaningful ways. Thus race relations remained relatively peaceful because, apart from some laws affecting land, kauri felling and customs payments, the governors did not try too much to impose their will on Maori. This changed in 1845 with the arrival of George Grey, who set about buying up large amounts of land from Maori. By 1865 just 1% of the South Island remained in Maori ownership. Still, initially Pakeha authority did not much affect Maori beyond a few populated areas such as Nelson, Whanganui and Auckland. For their part, the increasing number of settlers, mostly agricultural labourers encouraged here by the government, had no desire to be ruled by an unelected governor, much less so by Maori. They wanted to be able to elect their own government from among themselves, and in 1852 Britain granted them this right. The power of the governor (and thus, the British Crown) was greatly restricted; the 'covenant', it seemed, had ended. Few Maori were eligible to vote in the new parliament that sat for the first time in 1854. It thus reflected settler interests, which mostly meant getting hold of (Maori) land as cheaply as possible. By 1858 the settler population of 59,000 passed that of Maori (56,000), and it was growing at a much greater rate; these numbers represented a change in the political balance of power.

George Grey

2) In 1858, Waikato Maori and their supporters formed their own **political** organisation, the Kingitanga, a move that was seen as a threat by the government. A king, Potatau Te Wherowhero, was appointed from amongst the mostly central North Island tribes. His main responsibility was to look after

 ISBN: 9780170418393

Potatau Te Whero Whero

the lands and interests of the people. Such an organisation was quite in line with Maori understanding of Articles 1 and 2 of the Treaty, which they believed had established a partnership, but the settler government saw it as an illegal threat. In the early 1860s around 10,000 British soldiers were brought in to impose Crown authority, defeating the numerically smaller Kingitanga forces, despite some surprisingly stiff resistance. With the ability of Maori to oppose the government by military means curtailed *[decreased]*, the settler parliament was able to break further resistance through the use of the law, such as the Native Lands Acts, which undermined communal land ownership. By the end of the century, Maori rangatiratanga (political authority) had all but disappeared except for in a few remote areas, such as Aotea (Great Barrier Island). There were, however, vigorous efforts to keep it alive, including the formation of two Maori parliaments, Kotahitanga and Kauhanganui. Both focused on the Treaty and the government's obligation to honour it.

3) Although **military** conflict was not common, wars did occur in Northland in 1845 and, most significantly, in the central North Island in the 1860s. Hone Heke and his ally Kawiti were deeply disappointed that the trade benefits that the Treaty had seemed to offer had not materialised. Indeed, economically things had got worse, especially when Governor Hobson relocated the capital to Auckland. In 1845, dissatisfaction with this situation broke out into conflict when Heke repeatedly chopped down the flagstaff at Kororareka (Russell). Despite bringing in over 500 troops from Australia, Governor FitzRoy and then Grey could not defeat Heke and Kawiti, but nor could Heke and Kawiti defeat the British. A truce and then peace was agreed. While neither side was victorious in this conflict, the main wars of the 1860s (in Taranaki and the Waikato) resulted in an eventual loss for the numerically inferior Maori forces. Their problems were compounded by being a part-time force that still had to grow and harvest crops while flighting against a full-time army that was bigger and much better armed. For example, 500 Maori faced 1400 British troops at Rangiriri in November 1863. Still, this was no easy victory for the Crown. While the defeat of the Kingitanga forces marked the end of major engagements, several

ISBN: 9780170418393

other significant guerrilla wars continued to plague the east and west coasts of the North Island, involving Te Kooti and Titokowaru respectively. The government struggled to contain these skilled fighters but eventually prevailed *[triumphed]*. By 1872, the last shots of the New Zealand Wars had been fired and Maori military resistance was at an end.

4) **Economically**, Maori were dominant in New Zealand up until the late 1850s, especially in the North Island. In a variety of places such as Waikato they had vast fields of crops, which helped to feed the new settlements, including Auckland. The politician William Swainson described extensive farming activity amongst Te Arawa, Tuwharetoa and Mataatua iwi. By the early 1850s Maori dominated not only food production but also the coastal shipping that transported the goods to the settlements. Exports to the Australian and Californian goldfields extended their reach further. Flour mills to grind wheat for bread were common features of the Maori landscape, such as at Whanganui, Rotorua and Wairarapa. However, an economic slump in the mid-1850s and then the wars of the 1860s dealt Maori a severe economic blow. After the wars of the 1860s, up to four million acres of fertile Maori land were confiscated, leaving many hapu destitute *[in poverty]*. While the confiscations affected only Maori in certain areas, laws affecting land ownership affected all Maori. Between 1872 and 1900, some eight million acres of land shifted into Pakeha ownership. By 1939, Maori held only about 9% of the land in New Zealand, and much of that was low quality or mountainous – land the settler government did not want. Whereas Maori had been economically dominant in 1840, by 1900 they had lost most of their fertile land and with it their economic base. Conversely, the settlers benefited from this transfer of land from Maori to themselves. Notwithstanding *[despite]* a global recession throughout the 1880s and into the 1890s, for settlers by the end of the century, the economy was booming.

ISBN: 9780170418393

5) As Maori political and economic fortunes declined, along with their population, so too did their **culture**. Anyone arriving in New Zealand in 1840 would have had no doubts that they were in a Maori country. By 1900, disease, war and loss of land had decimated Maori. From an estimated population of 90,000 in 1840 there were around 42,000 Maori by 1900. (In contrast, the settler population was around 750,000 by 1900.) Alcohol, debt, and efforts by the government to convert Maori into 'brown Pakeha' through education in the Pakeha system had all taken their toll too. This is not to say that all Maori communities were unable to maintain their traditions, but poverty and disease did make this difficult. Those who lived in remote areas away from Pakeha settlements, fared best and were able to resist change the longest. Nevertheless, someone arriving in the country in 1900 would have been convinced that they were in a British-based country that contained a few isolated pockets of Maori, 'out of sight and out of mind' in remote areas such as Urewera and the Coromandel peninsula.

Short-term consequences	Long-term consequences

Explain why you 'drew the line' between short and long term consequences where you did.

11 ACTIVITY

Prioritising consequences

1 Using only the text on pages 82–85, which one or two consequences do you think were the **most significant** for **Maori**? Give your reasons.

2 Using only the text on pages 82–85, which one or two consequences do you think were the **most significant** for **Britain** and/or the **settlers**? Give your reasons.

- **Share your views with others in the class.**

Linking causes to consequences

As noted earlier, historians are keen to explore the links between what motivated people to take some action (in this case, entering into the Treaty) and the outcomes. Were the expectations met?

12 ACTIVITY

Refer to the 'Consequences of signing the Treaty of Waitangi, up to 1900' text on pages 81–85. In the left-hand columns of the chart on the next page are the key reasons why both Britain and Maori entered into the Treaty. (You may wish to also refer back to pages 66–72.)

- In the right-hand column, note down briefly any evidence you can find that shows whether the expectation in the left-hand column was met.
  - You might find that the expectation was fully met, met in the short-term, met in the long-term, not met at all, or it may not be clear (the text may not mention it).
  - Perhaps it could be some combination of these; for example, fully met in the short-term but not in the long-term. You decide!
- Provide evidence from the text where appropriate to support your response.

Note: For the purposes of this activity, we will be looking only up to the year 1900.

ISBN: 9780170418393

A. British expectations behind presenting Maori with the Treaty

If you need to, refer back to pages 66–68 to review more fully why Britain presented a Treaty to Maori.

Britain wanted to:	• **Did signing achieve this goal?** Provide evidence from the text where appropriate. • **Was the expectation met?** Fully/short-term/long-term/not at all/unclear?
A become the sole sovereign, with full authority to govern	
B curb the lawlessness that was impacting on trade and threatening investments	
C spread British ways of living across New Zealand	
D oversee the inflow of settlers into the country	
E prevent the New Zealand Company from establishing 'independent republics' beyond British law	
F keep possible rivals (France especially) from taking over	

ISBN: 9780170418393

Prioritising consequences

Review your response to Activity 11, question 2, on page 86. Which one or two consequences do you now think were the most significant for Britain/settlers? Give your reasons. If you have not changed your view, explain why not.

B. Main reasons why many Maori signed up to the Treaty

Refer back to pages 70–72 to review more fully why many Maori chiefs signed the Treaty.

The Maori chiefs who signed wanted to:	• **Did signing achieve this goal?** Provide evidence from the text where appropriate. • **Was the expectation met?** Fully/short-term/long-term/not at all/unclear?
A curb the lawlessness that was impacting on trade	
B increase trading opportunities	
C continue the positive relationship with Britain that extended back decades	
D not miss out on any of the benefits that other hapu might get by signing	

 ISBN: 9780170418393

The Maori chiefs who signed wanted to:	• **Did signing achieve this goal?** Provide evidence from the text where appropriate. • **Was the expectation met?** Fully/short-term/long-term/not at all/unclear?
E establish a 'sacred bond' between themselves and the Queen (British Crown)	
F have their rangatiratanga (chiefly authority) guaranteed	

Prioritising consequences

Review your response to Activity 11, question 1, on page 86. Which one or two consequences do you now think were the most significant for Maori? Give your reasons. If you have not changed your view, explain why not.

Unintended consequences

What we can see here with the Treaty is that there were a number of intended consequences; that is, the outcome that had been expected or hoped for actually happened. There were also plenty of consequences that Maori, especially, did not intend. However, when we speak of *unintended consequences*, we usually mean *unexpected consequences*, ones that the people involved might not have even thought about. Maori certainly did think about the risk of Britain trying to impose its authority on them and the subsequent loss of their lands, but they were (mostly) convinced by Hobson, the missionaries and other Europeans that this would not happen. The fact that this actually *did* happen was not so much an unintended consequence as an *unlikely consequence* given the assurances that they had received.

An excellent example of *unintended consequences* is the assassination in 1914 of the Austrian Archduke, Franz Ferdinand, in Sarajevo by the Bosnian terrorist/freedom-fighter Gavrilo Princip. This event was the 'trigger' or immediate cause of what would become World War I. However, Princip's action was intended just to 'convince' the imperial power Austria-Hungary that it should get out of his homeland; he had no idea that he would spark a global conflict that would cost some 17 million lives and bring about the downfall of three great Empires (and severely weaken a fourth, the British Empire). Before his death in 1918, Princip stated that if he had known what the terrible consequences would be, he would never have carried out the assassination.

ISBN: 9780170418393

Historical relationship: Intent and motivation

'Intent and motivation' looks at why in the past people acted the way they did. It requires us to understand the nature of the society in which they lived, including the political, social, technological and economic structures of the times. Following on from this, it requires us to understand the perspectives of the people who lived in those times and who had their values influenced by those structures. When we do this we can better understand what motivated people and what were their intentions. The historical relationship of 'intent and motivation' thus links closely to 'causes' (see pages 62-79).

As the subtitle of this workbook states, 'the past is another country' and it is a 'country' that we need to get to know if our study of it is to be valid. Something historians try to avoid at all costs is the transference of our modern values back to people in the past – this is called 'presentism'. We cannot assume that the way we think and feel today is the same as the way people thought and felt in the past. Nor should we allow ourselves to judge those in the past by our own values, especially if we find their views, beliefs or actions repugnant *[offensive]*. For example, it is all too easy to condemn southern segregationists in 1950s America as racist and leave it at that. However, the good historian will put aside whatever feelings they may have and explore the intent and motivation of such people further. Behind the outward display of racism they will find a more complex set of values encompassing religious beliefs, political issues, economic factors, culture (the 'Southern way') and fear. Attaching the label 'racist' to segregationists would thus be far too simplistic and 'presentist'.

Historical relationship: Contingency

Contingency can best be defined by what it isn't: inevitability. We can sometimes fall into the trap of thinking that things happened in the past simply because... that's just the way it was. However, whenever people in the past have taken actions there has almost always been choices or alternatives, even if not necessarily obvious or easy ones. In other words, things didn't have to happen or turn out the way they did. Like intent and motivation, contingency is most closely associated with the historical relationship of 'cause', particularly 'agency versus structure' (see page 76). It is also another way of thinking about the relative significance of a variety of causes. If, for example, Kate Sheppard had stood down as leader of the suffrage movement before the 1893 petition, would women have won the vote? If one of her deputies had instead stood down would this have affected the outcome? If the answer is 'yes' to the first question but 'unlikely' to the second, this would seem to show that Kate Sheppard's role was more significant.

As the above example suggests, one way to explore the idea of contingency is through 'counter-factual history'; in other words: 'What if...?'. A favourite example is the assassination of Hitler: what would have happened in Germany and beyond if he had been killed? There were ten attempts on his life between 1933 and 1944 and the 'answer' to this question would depend upon which attempt we looked at, as Hitler's power was much less assured in 1933 than it was later on. A number of historians have lain out possible 'alternative pasts' based on this question. Prominent British historian Niall Ferguson is an advocate of 'counter-factual' histories as a means to help us reject inevitability and explore the idea of contingency. Other historians are not so charitable, seeing such 'histories' as entertaining at best.

ISBN: 9780170418393

9 Historical relationship: Specific and general

You may be required to comment on the historical relationship of 'specific and general' when analysing a source; you will certainly use this relationship when you write a paragraph, whether you realise it or not. Specific information will appear in your paragraphs as evidence/examples. This makes sense when you recall that a paragraph always starts with a topic sentence, which is really just another name for a generalisation. The rest of the paragraph then explains the generalisation and backs it up with specific examples.

Here is a simple example from page 101 in *History Skills for NCEA Level 1*. You should refer to the rest of the section on paragraph writing for further examples of what in the end is really the historical relationship of 'specific and general'.

Specific points/examples/evidence

- Apples are pip fruit.
- Oranges are citrus fruit.
- Peaches and nectarines are called stone fruit.
- Even tomatoes are actually fruit!
- Different types of fruit grow best in different countries.

Corresponding generalisation

There are many different types of fruit.

As you probably know by now, historians will not make a generalisation based on only one or two specific pieces of evidence. The more evidence that supports a generalisation, the better!

1 ACTIVITY

Refer to the 'Consequences of signing the Treaty of Waitangi, up to 1900' text below (it is the same text as that on pages 82–85).

1 Highlight the topic sentence/generalisation for each paragraph.
2 Highlight the specific examples that back up the generalisation.

The last paragraph has been done for you as an exemplar.

GENERALISATION

Exemplar: Specific and general

As Maori political and economic fortunes declined, along with their population, so too did their culture. Anyone arriving in New Zealand in 1840 would have had no doubts that they were in a Maori country. By 1900, disease, war and loss of land had decimated Maori. From an estimated population of 90,000 in 1840 there were around 42,000 Maori by 1900. (In contrast, the settler population was around 750,000 by 1900.) Alcohol, debt, and efforts by the government to convert Maori to 'brown Pakeha' through education in the Pakeha system had all taken their toll too. This is not to say that all Maori communities were unable to maintain their traditions, but poverty and disease did make this difficult. Those who lived in remote areas away from Pakeha settlements fared best and were able to resist change the longest. Nevertheless, someone arriving in the country in 1900 would have been convinced that they were in a British-based country that contained a few isolated pockets of Maori, 'out of sight and out of mind' in remote areas such as Urewera and the Coromandel peninsula.

SPECIFICS

Consequences of signing the Treaty of Waitangi, up to 1900

1) Politically, after the signing of the Treaty the British Crown believed itself to be the sole governing authority, although power soon shifted from the governor to a settler parliament. William Hobson died in 1842 and was replaced by Robert FitzRoy, who in turn was replaced in 1845 by George Grey, the most influential of all the governors. The reality was, though, that while the settlers immediately came under British authority, the governors at first could do very little without the compliance *[agreement]* of Maori, who were still dominant in all meaningful ways. Thus race relations remained relatively peaceful because, apart from some laws affecting land, kauri felling and customs payments, the governors did not try too much to impose their will on Maori. This changed in 1845 with the arrival of George Grey, who set about buying up large amounts of land from Maori. By 1865 just 1% of the South Island remained in Maori ownership. Still, initially Pakeha authority did not much affect Maori beyond a few populated areas such as Nelson, Whanganui and Auckland. However, the increasing number of settlers, mostly agricultural labourers encouraged her by the government, had no desire to be ruled by an unelected governor, much less so by Maori. They wanted to be able to elect their own government from among themselves and in 1852 Britain granted them this right. The power of the governor (and thus, the British Crown) was greatly restricted; the 'covenant', it seemed, had ended. Few Maori were eligible to vote in the new parliament that sat for the first time in 1854. It thus reflected settler interests, which mostly meant getting hold of (Maori) land as cheaply as possible. By 1858 the settler population of 59,000 passed that of Maori (56,000), and it was growing at a much greater rate; these numbers represented a change in the political balance of power.

2) In 1858 Waikato Maori and their supporters formed their own political organisation, the Kingitanga, but this move was seen as a threat by the government. A king, Potatau Te Wherowhero, was appointed from among the mainly central North Island tribes. His main responsibility was to look after the lands and interests of the people. Such an organisation was quite in line with Maori understanding of Articles 1 and 2 of the Treaty, which established a partnership, but the settler government saw it as an illegal threat. In the early 1860s around 10,000 British soldiers were brought in to impose Crown authority, defeating the numerically smaller Kingitanga forces and some surprisingly stiff resistance. With the ability of Maori to oppose the government by military means curtailed [decreased], the settler parliament was able to break further resistance through the use of the law, such as the Native Lands Acts, which broke communal land ownership. By the end of the century, Maori rangatiratanga (political authority) had all but disappeared except for in a few remote areas, such as Aotea (Great Barrier Island). There were, however, vigorous efforts to keep it alive, including the formation of two Maori parliaments, Kotahitanga and Kauhanganui. Both focused on the Treaty and the government's obligation to honour it.

  ISBN: 9780170418393

3) Although military conflict was not common, wars did occur in Northland in 1845 and, most significantly, in the central North Island in the 1860s. Hone Heke and his ally Kawiti were deeply disappointed that the trade benefits that the Treaty had seemed to offer had not materialised. Indeed, economically things had got worse, especially when Governor Hobson relocated the capital to Auckland. In 1845, dissatisfaction with this situation broke out into conflict when Heke repeatedly chopped down the flagstaff at Kororareka (Russell). Despite bringing in over 500 troops from Australia, Governor FitzRoy and then Grey could not defeat Heke and Kawiti, but nor could Heke and Kawiti defeat the British. A truce and then peace was agreed. As noted, the main wars of the 1860s (in Taranaki and the Waikato) resulted in an eventual loss for the numerically inferior Maori forces. Their problems were compounded by being a part-time force that still had to grow and harvest crops while up against a full-time army that was bigger and much better armed. For example, 500 Maori faced 1400 British troops at Rangiriri in November 1863. Still, this was no easy victory for the Crown. While the defeat of the Kingitanga forces marked the end of major engagements, several other significant guerrilla wars continued to plague the east and west coasts of the North Island, involving Te Kooti and Titokowaru respectively. The government struggled to contain these skilled fighters but eventually prevailed *[triumphed]*. By 1872, the last shots of the New Zealand Wars had been fired and Maori military resistance was at an end.

4) Economically, Maori were dominant in New Zealand up until the late 1850s, especially in the North Island. In a variety of places such as Waikato they had vast fields of crops, which helped to feed the new settlements such as Wellington and New Plymouth and literally kept them alive in the early post-Treaty years. The politician William Swainson described extensive farming activity among Te Arawa, Tuwharetoa and Mataatua iwi. By the early 1850s Maori dominated food production and the coastal shipping that got the goods to the settlements. Exports to the Australian and Californian goldfields extended their reach further. Flour mills to grind wheat for bread were common features of the Maori landscape, such as at Whanganui, Rotorua and Wairarapa. However, an economic slump in the mid-1850s and then the wars of the 1860s dealt Maori a severe economic blow. After the wars of the 1860s, up to four million acres of fertile Maori land were confiscated, leaving many hapu destitute *[in poverty]*. While the confiscations affected only Maori in certain areas, laws affecting land ownership affected all Maori. Between 1872 and 1900, some eight million acres of land shifted into Pakeha ownership. By 1939, Maori held only about 9% of the land in New Zealand, and much of that was low quality or mountainous – land the settler government did not want. Whereas Maori had been economically dominant in 1840, by 1900 they had lost most of their fertile land and with it their economic base. Conversely, the settlers benefited from this transfer of land from Maori to themselves. Notwithstanding *[despite]* a global recession throughout the 1880s and into the 1890s, for settlers by the end of the century the economy was booming.

Note that in a source analysis activity in an exam situation, you may be required to determine the generalisation yourself from the specific evidence; it may not be conveniently located in the topic sentence.

10 Historical relationship: Past and present

The historical relationship (or concept) of 'past and present' is in many ways an extension of 'cause and consequence'. The key difference is that the links between an event or situation in the past are detected up to the present day (or near-present day). Sometimes these links have persisted through time, even if not always very visibly, and could thus be described as 'very long term and ongoing consequences'. In other instances these effects might seem to disappear entirely only to reappear many years, decades or even centuries later. As always, historians will debate the nature of this historical relationship.

Example of the historical relationship of 'past and present'

An example of 'past and present' can be found in the outcome of the US Civil War (1861-65) and modern issues around the commemoration of that conflict. The war was a result of increasing tension between the northern and southern US states. The economy and thinking of the north was based in large part around modern ideas and industrialisation; by contrast, the economy and way of life in the south was based on agriculture (especially cotton) on large plantations worked by slaves. Eventually the southern states, feeling threatened by the growing anti-slavery mood, decided to break away from the Union of States. In response, the north went to war against them to maintain the Union, finally defeating the South after four years of brutal and costly fighting. The bitterness of the South towards the North did not suddenly end when they were defeated; nor did the racist attitudes of whites towards blacks, despite the emancipation *[freeing]* of slaves in 1863. Within a decade of the end of the war, whites began to reassert their authority over blacks through the law and also by the use of terror. (See page 49 for more on this.)

During the war, one of the key military men in the South was General Robert E. Lee. He became a capable enough military leader and his reputation grew with each of his victories; however, many of these were due to the sheer incompetence of the northern generals he was up against. In terms of his views on slavery, Lee had inherited a few slaves from his mother and then married into a wealthy slave-holding family. Documents show that he was a cruel slaveholder; he encouraged his overseers to severely beat slaves captured after trying to escape. One slave said Lee was one of the meanest men she had ever met. After the Civil War southerners wanted to build memorials to honour Lee's military leadership but he refused, saying instead that the nation must put the conflict behind them. After his death, however, Lee became a central icon of resurgent *[reviving]* southern white pride, exemplified *[shown]* by the boost in membership of the KKK. Monuments to commemorate Lee went up in a number of places, including one in 1924 in Charlottesville, Virginia.

Although the civil rights movement, with Martin Luther King as a notable leader, succeeded in ending the worst of the South's racist laws in the 1960s, it was not until more recent times that attention was turned to the memorials that had become icons for southern racists: thus **past and present**. The pressure to remove such monuments was partly a response to violent acts committed by white supremacists using southern Civil War symbols as rallying points. For example, in 2015 white supremacist Dylann Roof shot and killed

  ISBN: 9780170418393

nine black worshippers in their church in South Carolina. In 2017 the Charlottesville City Council voted to remove its Lee statue from a city park, sparking a lawsuit from opponents of the move. White supremacists also called a demonstration to defend the Lee statue, and violence broke out as counter-demonstrators confronted them. One person was killed and many more were injured.

Analysis: Past and present

We can see the historical relationship of 'past and present' in action here between the attitudes of southern whites in the Civil War period (and beyond) and the modern reaction against attempts to remove from public places those monuments that commemorate the southern cause. Furthermore, when we consider the long-term background of slavery in America and the different attitudes towards it, we can see that the concept/historical relationship of 'past and present' is not the only relevant one here. There is also plenty of evidence of both continuity and change, as well as cause and consequences. This is how history works; it is rarely, if ever, simplistic. This is why the critical thinking skills involved are of a high order.

1 ACTIVITY

'Past and present'

Study the two events below; one is from the past while a related one is from the present (or near present). Explain the link between these two distinct events, even though they are separated by a significant period of time.

- You *might* also like to consider in your thinking the related historical relationship of cause/consequence and perhaps even continuity/change. You may also bring in your own knowledge, but be sure that it is factual.
- You can also note any questions that the sources may raise in your mind.

1

Past	Present (or near present)
Background *The Treaty of Waitangi (1840) was understood by Maori to be some sort of power-sharing relationship between chiefs and the Crown, but the Crown believed that it had full authority.* **Event** Invasion of the Waikato by British troops. Defeat of the Kingitanga forces, 1863–64. Confiscation of millions of acres of 'rebel' Maori land. *(Refer to pages 82–85 for more information on this.)*	**'National day to remember the New Zealand Wars to start in 2017'** *Stuff news*, 31 October 2016 A national day marking the 19th-century New Zealand Wars has been set: 28 October. It is same day as the signing of the 1835 Declaration of Independence. The first commemoration day, in 2017, will be hosted by the Te Taitokerau tribes in Northland. After that, the commemorations will move from year to year to recognise battle sites around the country. Six years have passed since Otorohanga College students Leah Bell and Waimarama Anderson mooted the idea of a day to recognise the wars after a school trip to the Orakau battle site near Kihikihi, Waikato. They started a petition calling for a commemoration day, presented 12,000 signatures to Parliament in December 2015 and have finally been rewarded for their effort. 'Each battle has its own story to tell and a national commemoration day will help in sharing that story with the whole country,' they said. The aim of the petition was to raise awareness of the Land Wars and to introduce the history in the national curriculum.

Critical thinking skills

ISBN: 9780170418393

- Explain the link here between past and present.
  You may also wish to refer to the Anzac Day article below.

2

Past	Present (or near present)
Background *On April 25th 1915 New Zealand and Australians troops (Anzacs) landed on Gallipoli peninsula as part of the Allied campaign to access the Black Sea and knock Turkey out of the war. Among the dead in this disastrous attack were 2779 New Zealanders, about a sixth of those who served.* **Event** On 30 April 1915, when the first news of the landing reached New Zealand, a half-day holiday was declared and spontaneous services were held. The date 25 April was officially named Anzac Day in 1916 and it became a public holiday in 1920.	**'Anzac Day 2015: NZ marks 100th Gallipoli anniversary'** *Newshub*, 24 April 2015 This year's Anzac Day is being heralded as one of the biggest yet, with thousands of Kiwis today marking the 100th anniversary of the Gallipoli campaign.... Among the ceremonies scheduled nationwide, people young and old flocked to the Dawn Service at the new Pukeahu National War Memorial in Wellington, with an estimated 20,000 filling the park's concourse for the moving ceremony. In Auckland, a crowd of 34,000 gathered at the War Memorial Museum, easily exceeding the previous record of 20,000, and big numbers were also reported in Dunedin and Christchurch. Historian Dr Jock Phillips said he recalls a time in the 1980s when there was 'simply no interest' in WWI. 'There's been a quite extraordinary revival of interest, and it's fascinating that has happened,' he says. Returned Services Association (RSA) chief executive David Moger expected 'some very substantial crowds' today. 'Based upon the feedback and conversations we're getting, I think this Anzac Day will be the biggest in our history. Anzac Day is a day when we commemorate and remember the service and sacrifice of those who built the foundation of our nation, but also all those since that have served and given us the freedoms that we enjoy today.'

- Explain the link here between past and present.
  You may also wish to refer to the New Zealand Wars Day article on page 95.

ISBN: 9780170418393

3 Explain the link here between past and present.

Past	Present (or near present)
Background *The campaign for women's suffrage is successful, 1893. Women win the right to stand for Parliament in 1919, and in 1933 Elizabeth McCombs becomes the first woman MP.* **Event** Women's organisations campaign in the 1970s for equal pay; Equal Pay Act passed in 1972, making it illegal to pay women less when doing the same job as men.	**'Historic pay increase for workers in female dominated industry'** *Stuff* news, 18 April 2017 The Government has announced a $2 billion package to address the pay inequity *[imbalance]* in the predominantly *[mainly]* female aged care sector. The deal will see more than 55,000 workers receive a minimum pay rise of $4 an hour, going up by as much as $7 an hour in some cases... and the Government hoped it would encourage businesses to make greater moves in addressing the overall gender pay gap in New Zealand.... The settlement is the result of the fight of one woman – Kristine Bartlett, an aged care worker from Lower Hutt... she argued in court in 2012 that her employer TerraNova was under-paying staff because of the high percentage of female employees... Her landmark Court of Appeal decision found women in predominantly female workforces could make a claim for pay equity under the Equal Pay Act, 1972.

4 Explain the link here between past and present.

Past	Present (or near present)
Background *From the 1970s, public opposition to French nuclear testing in the Pacific grew. By the 1980s this opposition spread to the visit of nuclear-armed (and even powered) warships. New Zealand had had a defence relationship with America (Anzus) since 1952 under which US warship visits were common.* **Event** In 1985, under its anti-nuclear policy, the Labour government refused to allow a routine visit of an American warship, as it would not confirm that it did not carry nuclear weapons. In response the US effectively ended the Anzus defence treaty. Relations between the two countries were strained. (National governments eventually accepted the nuclear ban due to strong public support for it.)	**'US warship USS *Sampson* heads to New Zealand'** *New Zealand Herald*, 18 October, 2016 The United States Navy is sending the *USS Sampson* to New Zealand, the first US warship to visit New Zealand in 33 years, after an invite from the New Zealand Navy. Prime Minister John Key said he had granted approval for the ship to visit to take part in the International Naval Review for the Navy's 75th birthday celebrations next month. Under New Zealand's anti-nuclear law, the Prime Minister has to be satisfied that any visiting ship is not nuclear armed or powered. 'I have granted this approval after careful consideration of the advice provided by the Ministry of Foreign Affairs and Trade,' he said. The law has never required foreign countries to confirm or deny whether their vessels are nuclear armed or powered. But the US decided that they would not send any more ships as part of the reprisals *['payback']* for the anti-nuclear policy. The process for considering the visit by the USS *Sampson* is the same as that used for all ships attending the International Naval Review. This process has been used for all military ships visiting New Zealand since the legislation was enacted....The visit is a further reflection of the depth of the bilateral *[two-way]* relationship with the United States,' Key said. While peace groups intend to have a small presence on the water when the USS *Sampson* arrives, there will be nothing like the 35,000 who turned out in 1983 to protest the arrival of the USS *Truxton*.

- Share you responses with others in the class when you have finished.

ISBN: 9780170418393

11 Analysing statistics and graphs

As students of history we are most used to dealing with text and, to a lesser extent, political cartoons and images. However, the Level 3 resource standard (AS3.3) notes that the types of sources that could appear in an exam paper include 'documents, pictures, *graphs*, *maps*, articles, speeches, cartoons, text books'. It is therefore important to know something about graph interpretation, including understanding how graphs are derived from statistics. (Interpreting maps will be dealt with in the next chapter.) As with all of the skills in History, the ability to critically examine statistics/graphs is also valuable for the citizen who is on the alert for misinformation. There are certainly those whose goal it is to deliberately mislead with statistics or graphic presentations, and the problem is not new. American writer Mark Twain claims that it was Benjamin Disraeli, British Prime Minister in the later 19th century, who memorably stated: *'There are three types of lies: lies, damn lies, and statistics.'* Thus, when dealing with statistics and their graphical representation we need to adopt the same approach as we do with sources of other types: healthy scepticism *[doubt]*.

Why we do 'sampling', according to Darrell Huff

'If you have a barrel of beans, some red and some white, there is only one way to find out exactly how many of each colour you have: count 'em. If it's a big barrel of beans, this could take a long time. However, you can find out approximately how many are red in much easier fashion by '**sampling**'; in other words, pulling out a handful of beans and counting just those, figuring that the proportion will be the same all through the barrel. If your sample is large enough and selected properly, it will represent the whole well enough for most purposes. If it is not, it may be far less accurate than an intelligent guess and have nothing to recommend it but a spurious *[unsupported]* air of scientific precision. It is a sad truth that conclusions from such samples, biased or too small or both, lie behind much of what we read or think we know.'

From: *How to Live with Statistics*

Statistics and graphs appear trustworthy by their nature: solid figures with mathematical precision, free of the taint of bias or misrepresentation. However, we must keep in mind that statistics are gathered and created by *people*. People choose what to count or measure, what method will be used to do the counting or measuring, which of the results from this process will be published, what form that publication will take, and what interpretation will be put on the results. Any time that people are involved in any part of this process there is room for bias to creep in, whether intentional or not.

Statistics

The plausibility test

Sometimes just a simple check of a statistical claim is enough to identify any problems. Here's an example. A number of years ago a newspaper report claimed: 'In the 35 years since marijuana laws stopped being enforced in California, the number of marijuana smokers has doubled every year.' Wow! This sounds pretty alarming; surely something needs to be done about this.

But take a moment to consider the report. Imagine at the start of the 35-year period there was just one marijuana smoker. Have a go now at doubling the number *every year for 35 years* – what do you get? At a total of over one billion marijuana smokers after 35 years of doubling, this is ... implausible! (California's entire population is only around 40 million.) Quick checks like this on the 'facts' can often expose silly claims.

Statistics checklist: Five basic questions to ask of a statistic

1. Who is collecting/presenting the figures? Look for bias, both intentional and unintentional. What benefit or effect (if any) is the data collector and/or publisher looking to achieve?
2. How does the collector know that their statistics are reliable? Is the method of data collection sound?
3. What's been omitted? What else might you have expected to see that has not been included?
4. Do the conclusions drawn really match the data? (There is a lot of room for different interpretations – even bias – here.)
5. On the face of it, does the outcome look plausible *[likely]*?

1 ACTIVITY

Statistics reliability

Refer to the table of statistics on lynching in the United States, pages 50–51.

1. Use some or all of the five questions in the statistics checklist (above) to guide your analysis of the figures presented. You may not be able to discover the answers to all of these questions, but at least you'll be thinking critically!

2. Refer to the text section 'The plausibility test' above. Are there any lynching statistics in the tables that seem to be out of line with the others? If so, note the nature of your queries about them.

When finished, share your responses with the rest of the class.

ISBN: 9780170418393

Collecting data: Issues with opinion polling

Opinion polling is a form of survey undertaken usually to understand how a group of people – often, but not always, the general public – is feeling about an issue. This is done by asking questions of a smaller cross-section of the group in an attempt to ascertain *[find out]* a sense of the wider views (see the boxed text on 'sampling', page 99). The first known example of an opinion poll was a local one conducted by *The Aru Pennsylvanian* newspaper during the presidential election in 1824, so it is entirely possible that you may come across one during research, or you could be required to analyse one in an exam situation. There are a few important issues you will need to know about to be able to analyse one thoughtfully.

The first major issue is with how the data is collected in the first place. The way that questions are phrased can have a significant impact on the way those being polled answer them. As data analyst Heiko Tröster says, 'specific wording patterns have a persuasive effect and cause respondents to answer in a predictable manner'. He points, by way of example, to a poll seeking opinions on taxation. Here are two potential questions:

- 'Do you believe that you should be taxed so other citizens don't have to work?'
- 'Do you think that the government should help those people who cannot find work?'

These two questions are likely to elicit *[obtain]* very different responses, even though they are dealing with the same topic of government assistance. These are examples of 'loaded questions'. A better way of framing the question so that it is neutral would be: 'What is your view of the government providing unemployment assistance?'

As Tröster concludes, a good approach is to always be sceptical of poll results unless you can see the questions that were actually asked. These will provide great insight, most often into the desired outcome of the organisation commissioning the polling. Darrell Huff, author of a book called *How to Lie with Statistics*, agrees with Tröster, saying that 'even if you can't find a source of demonstrable *[obvious]* bias, allow yourself some degree of scepticism about the results as long as there is a possibility of bias somewhere. There usually is.'

2 ACTIVITY

Here are four survey questions that have been worded poorly in order to achieve a certain outcome. Rewrite them so that they are neutral.

1 The leading question

Some survey questions are designed to sway responses to a particular side.

Leading question: 'Should responsible dog owners vaccinate their pets?'

Your neutral version: ______________________________

____

2 The loaded question

With the loaded question, people feel pressured into answering the question in a particular way.

Loaded question: 'Which punk rock band is your favourite?'

Your neutral version: ______________________________

____

ISBN: 9780170418393

3 The double-barrelled question

This forces respondents to try to answer two questions at once.

Double-barrelled question: 'How happy or unhappy are you with the rate of current funding for schools and the NCEA?'

Your neutral version: ______________________________

____

____

4 The absolute question

Yes or no answers can force respondents into making a choice that does not fully represent their views; without the opportunity to explain further the results may be distorted.

Absolute question: 'Do you always shower before bed?'

Your neutral version: ______________________________

____

Averages: Mean, median, mode

Many of us use the term 'average' fairly loosely. We usually know what we mean but if we're not clear on the differences between mean, median and mode, we can be tricked by those who want to mislead us.

$45,000

$15,000

$10,000

Mean average

$5,700

$5,000

$3,700

Median (the one in the middle, 12 above, 12 below)

$3,000

Mode (occurs most frequenty)

$2,000

Mean: This is what most of us actually … mean when we say 'average'. Given a set of values, the mean is what you get by adding up all of the values, and then dividing that sum by the number of values. This gives us a good general idea about the nature of a group of things. For example, the diagram shows a group of 25 people organised in order of their monthly salaries.

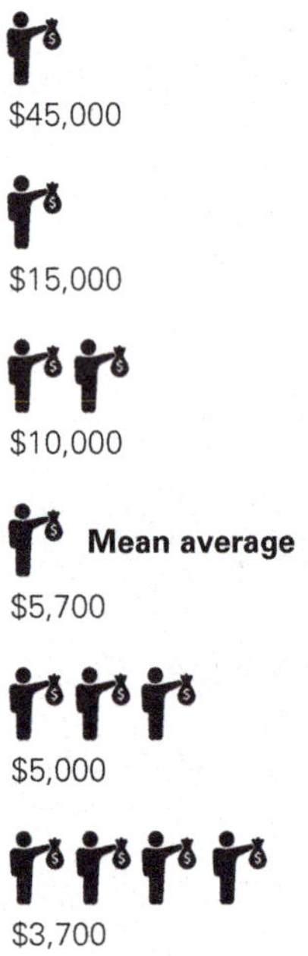

1 x $45,000 +
1 x $15,000 +
2 x $10,000 +
1 x $5,700 +
3 x $5,000 +
4 x $3,700 +
1 x $3,000 +
12 x $2,000
= $142,500

To find the mean:

- Begin by adding all of the values together; in this case the values are monthly salaries. The result in the example here is $142,500.
- Now, to find the mean/average, divide the total monthly salaries ($142,500) by all of the people in the group (25). The resulting mean/average is $5,700. By chance, there happens to be one of the group who earns this exact amount.

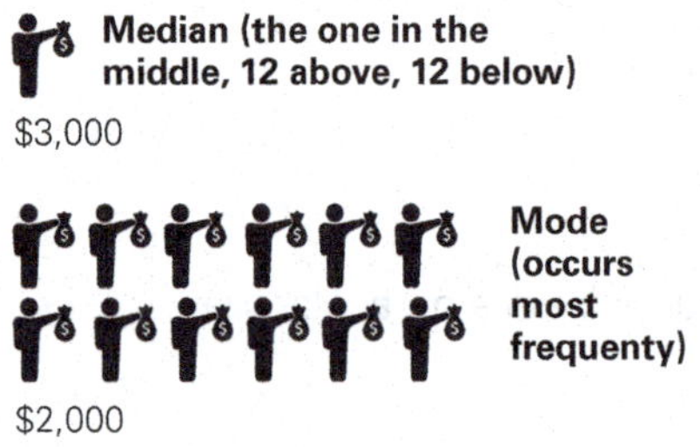

Median: This type of 'average' often gives us a better idea of a *typical* member of a group. If you take all of the values in a group and arrange them in increasing order, the number at the centre will be the **median**. If the group happened to be one that contained 29 students and we placed them in order of their birthdays, the median student (or students) would be number 15 in the line-up, with 14 students to the left and 14 to the right.

Mode: This type of 'average' means 'the most common member of the group'. For example, if five people all had a birthday on 4 March, and no other date had as many birthdays, then the **mode** is 4 March. It doesn't matter where in the birthday line-up this date comes – whatever value is *most common* is the **mode**. This measure of 'average' is least used because it's generally the least meaningful.

ISBN: 9780170418393

Graphs

At the most basic level, you should be able to describe the trend being shown in a graph. The diagram here gives some descriptors that you could use for data that is mostly in a linear *[straight-line]* relationship. To strengthen your analysis you should add in evidence from the graph at appropriate points; for example, at the beginning and end point of a linear progression. This might be something like: '*The number of young people aged 18–25 voting in elections increased steadily from 65% in 1989 to 75% in 2009.*' If there are significant changes in the shape of the graph, similar evidence should be provided at these points. Note that the 'increased steadily' in the example above is an interpretation and, like all interpretations, someone else analysing the graph might describe it differently.

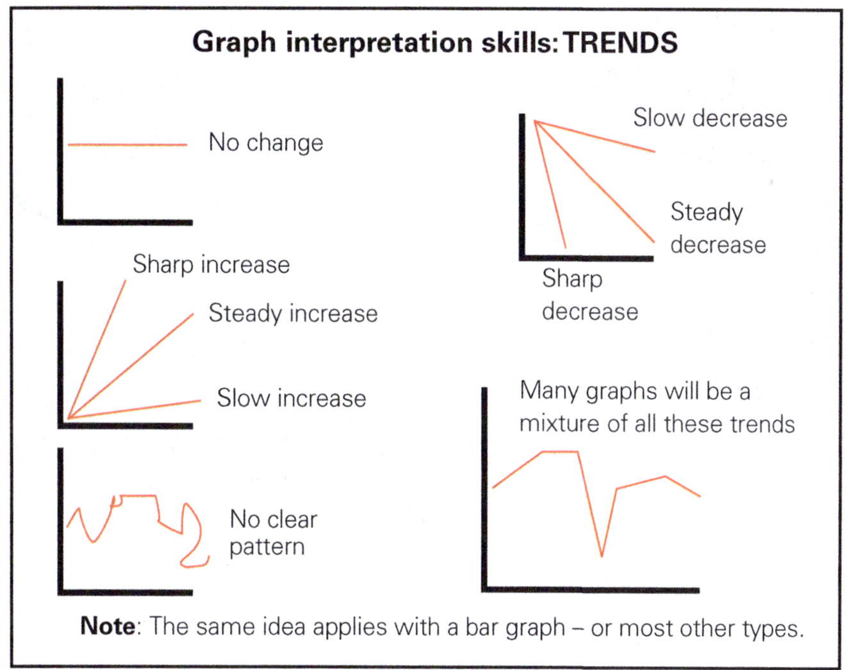

Exponential relationship

This graph shows an exponential relationship. In other words, the value on the y-axis increases exponentially (doubles, triples, etc.) with each increment on the x-axis.

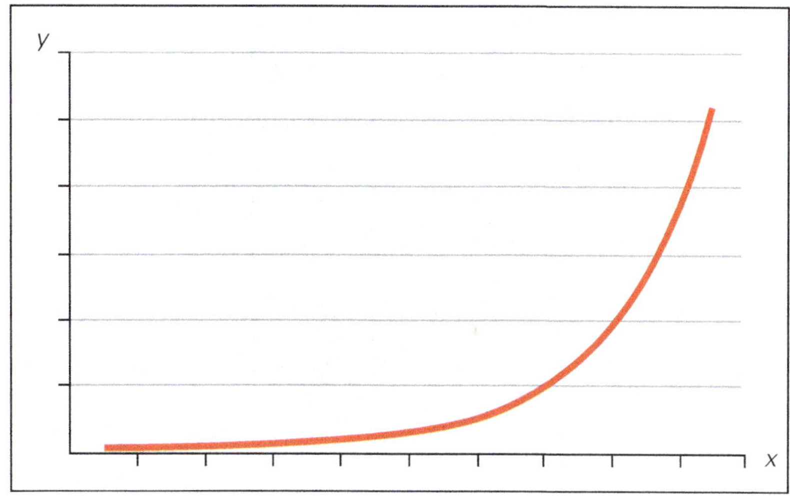

ISBN: 9780170418393

Simple pie chart

Pie charts always represent proportions and therefore all the segments together add up to 100% (= 360°) of a total. The total in the example above is the world's population. Each segment represents a different religious affiliation *['membership']*. If you add up all of the segment percentages, they should come to 100% (or very close; sometimes there is a slight discrepancy, but if there is, it should be explained). Every pie chart should have a title and each segment should be labelled.

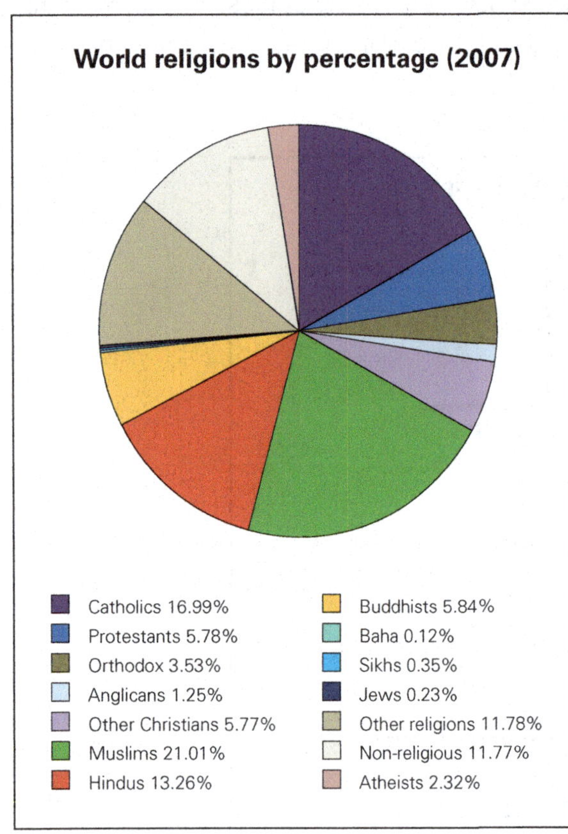

Be sure not to fall for the basic error that Fox News did in reporting on opinion polling for the GOP ('Grand Old Party' = Republicans) primaries. Oops! (Confused? Add up the percentages ...)

It is often useful to be able to estimate a proportion on a pie chart. The graphic below is a good guide.

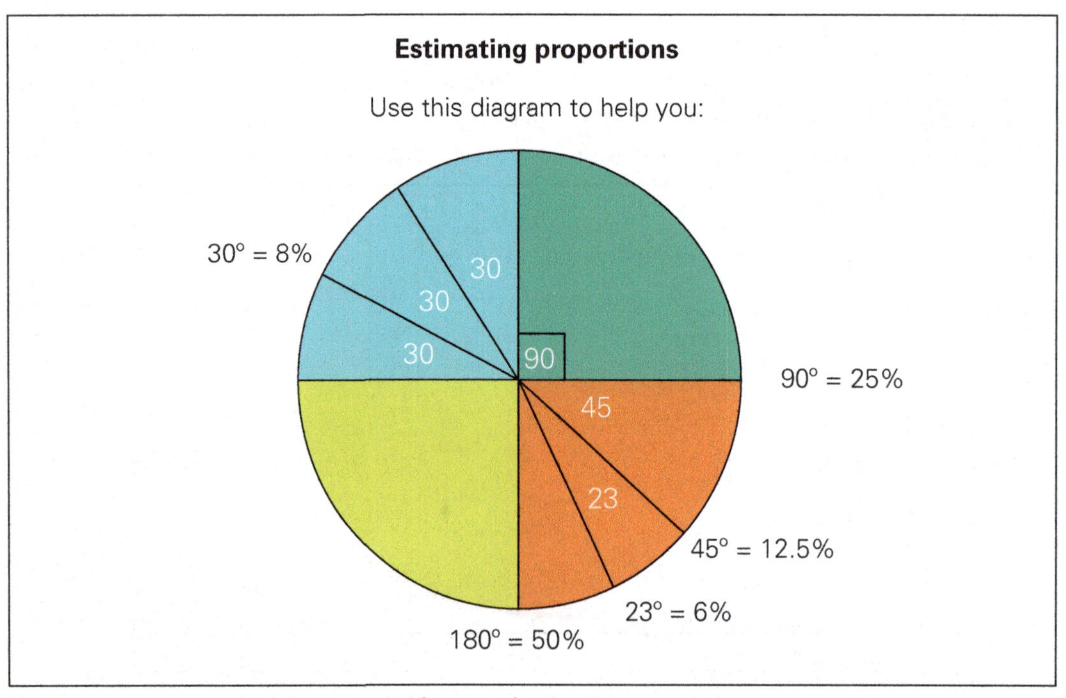

Note: some percentages have been rounded for ease of estimation.

ISBN: 9780170418393

3 ACTIVITY

Use the graphic guide on page 104 to estimate answers to the following questions. Refer to the appropriate pie charts. While these charts may not be specifically 'historical', they suit the point of the activities well.

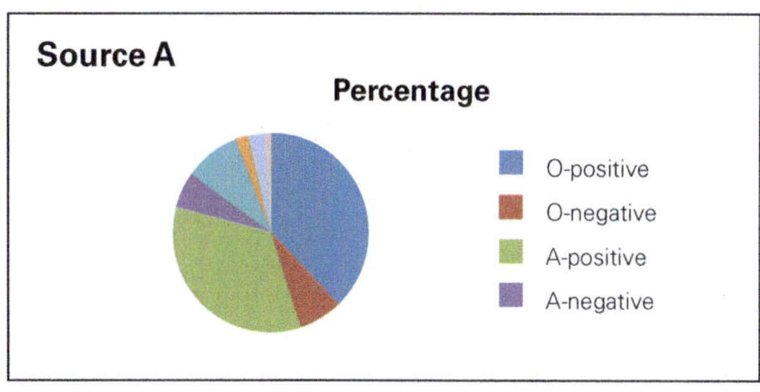

Source A: Approximately what percentage of the population has the following blood types?

a O-positive ____________

b O-negative ____________

c A-positive ____________

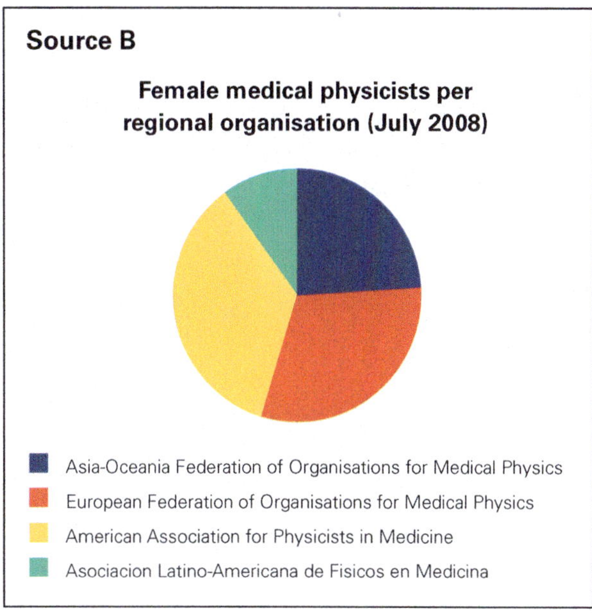

Source B: Approximately what percentage of female physicists is from:

a Asia-Oceania? ____________

b Europe? ____________

c (North) America? ____________

d Latin-America? ____________

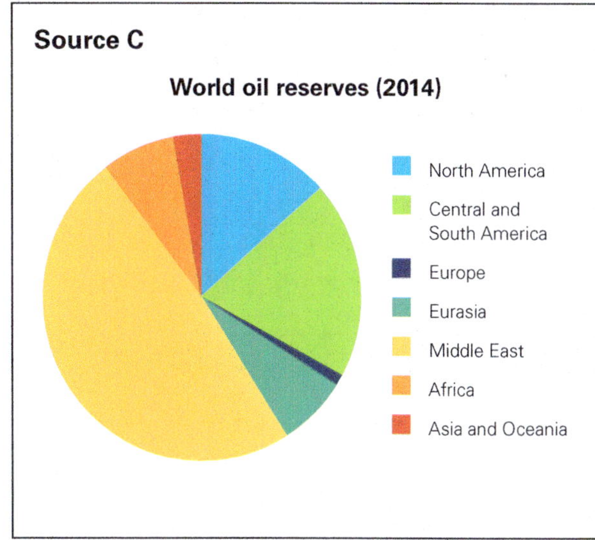

Source C: Approximately what percentage of the world's oil reserves are held in:

a North America? ____________

b Central/South America/ ____________

c Eurasia? ____________

d Middle East? ____________

e Africa? ____________

ISBN: 9780170418393

Refer to the guidelines on page 103. Provide two or three appropriate pieces of evidence from the graph in each of your responses.

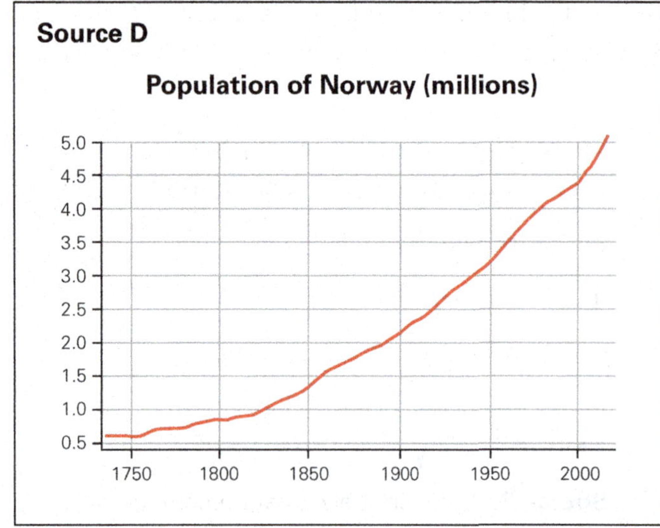

Source D: Describe the trend in the population of Norway, 1735–2014.

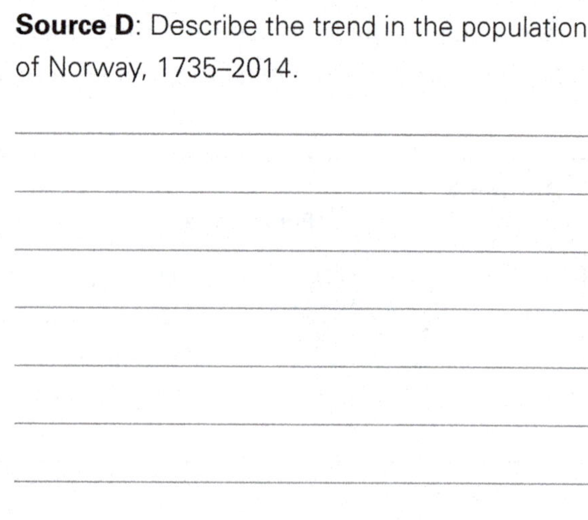

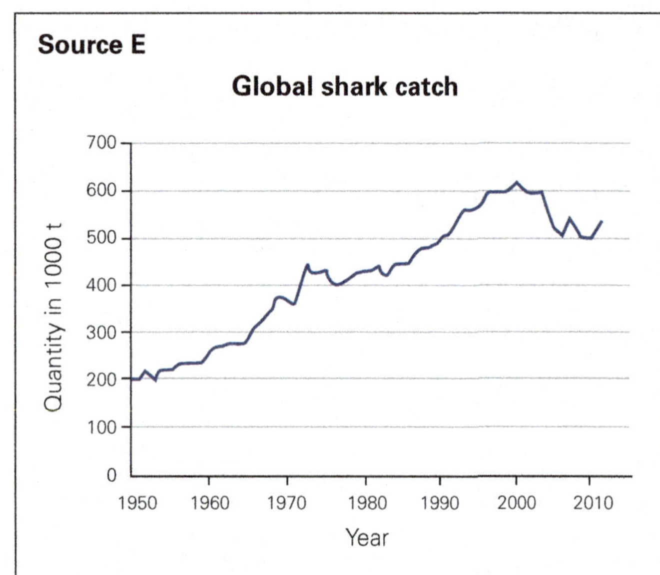

Source E: Describe the trend in the global shark catch, 1950–2010. (The *y*-axis is in 1000s of tonnes of catch.)

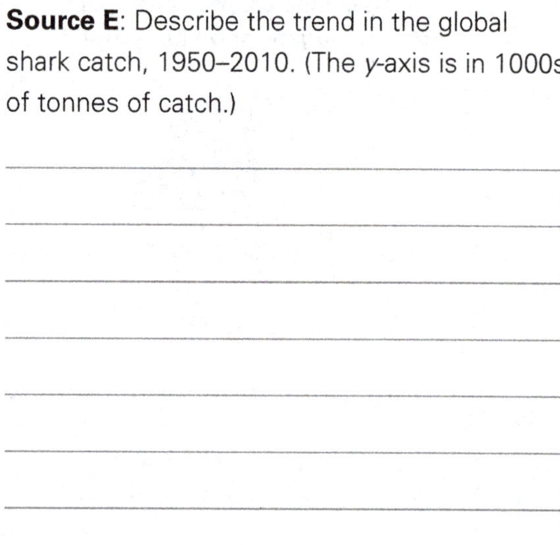

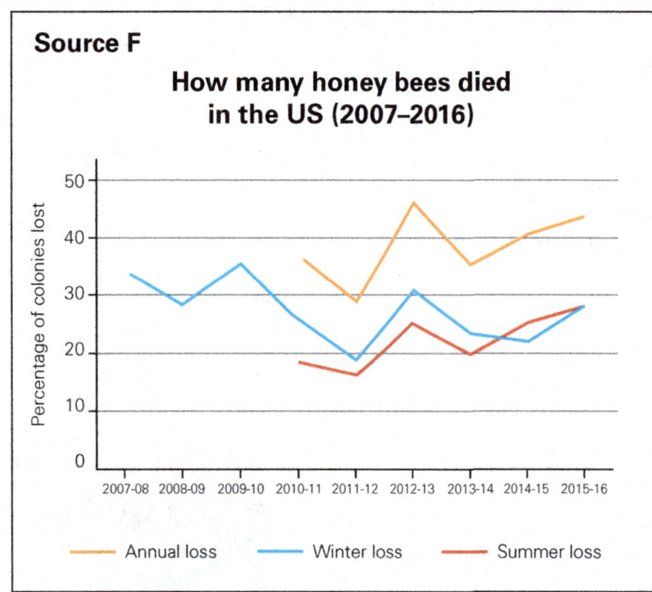

Source F: Describe the trends in each of the three sets of data on honey bee deaths.

 ISBN: 9780170418393

Graphs: Watching out for the traps

Ours brains have not evolved to process large amounts of numerical data presented in tables; instead our eyes look for patterns in data that are visually displayed. People who are trying to mislead us through otherwise 'reliable' graphs know how to play to the short-comings of our visual interpretation.

Trickery with shapes

Both of these pie charts show (American) 'Labor' (i.e. the workforce, not the political party) taking up 30% of some total. In which graph does 'Labor' make up the largest proportion? *(Circle one.)*

Example 1

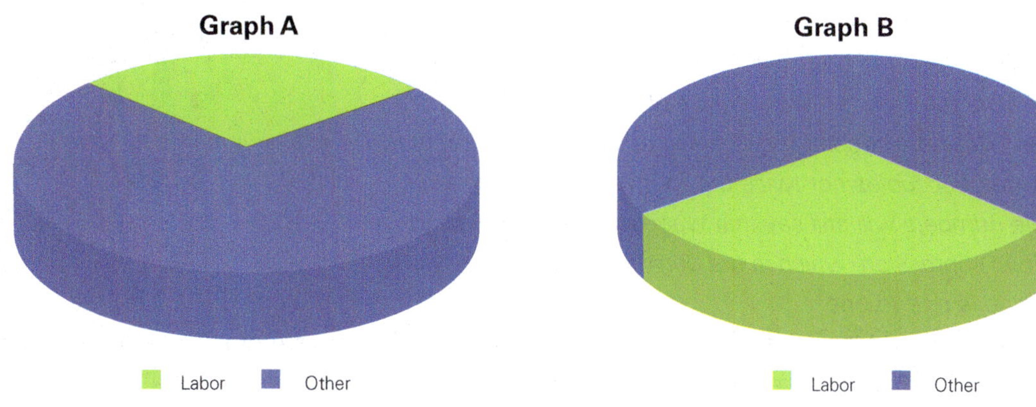

If you answered Graph B, you've fallen nicely for the trick being played on you. The chart on the right makes the 'Labor' slice look a lot bigger. It does this by positioning it in the foreground, which gives it a thick 3D (three-dimensional) edge and more than double the apparent size than when it's in the background. Human vision easily misinterprets 3D charts, says Massachusetts Institute of Technology perceptual scientist Ruth Rosenholtz. In both of these charts, 'Labor' actually represents the same one-third of the 'pie'.

In Example 2 is another use of shapes to deceive. Two different representations of the expenditure of a charitable educational organisation are shown. There are three main ways in which money is spent: Grants (such as scholarships), Research, and Administration (the costs of running the organisation).

For this organisation to continue to receive funding from wealthy donors, it needs to show that most of what it receives is used to achieve its educational purposes. It thus wants to spend as little as possible on administration. Failing this, it wants to *appear* to spend as little as possible on administration. Graph A helps do this, as the eye is irresistibly drawn to the large green base of the cone: 'Research' appears at a quick glance to be a huge part of what the organisation spends money on, and 'Administration' only a relatively small part.

Example 2

Graph A
Annual expenditure

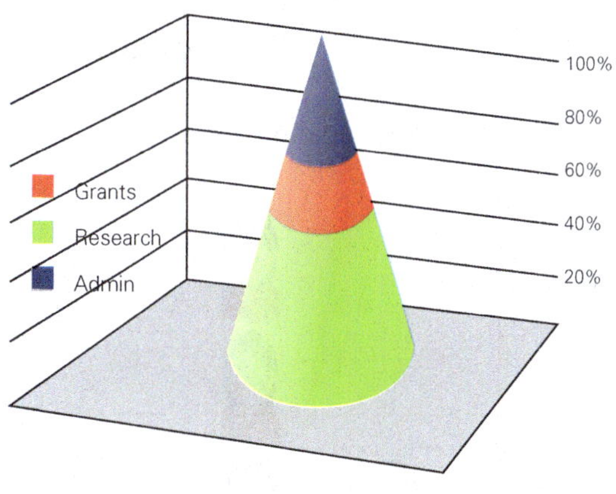

Graph B
Annual expenditure

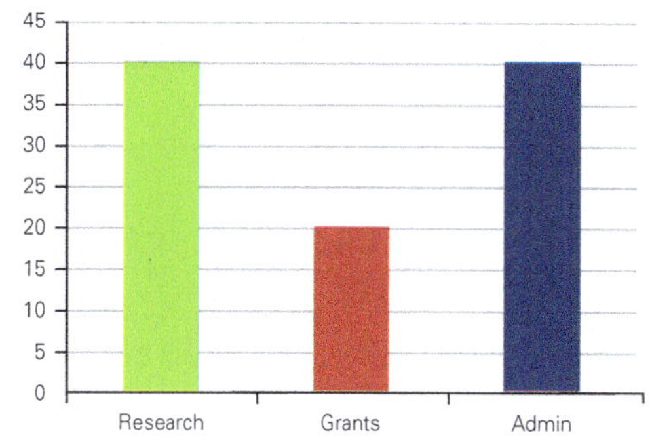

ISBN: 9780170418393

However, Graph B is a more 'honest' representation, so using the cone representation with its disproportionately large base is either dishonest or naive *[foolish]*. Perhaps this organisation felt that spending 40% of its income on administration was a bad look.

Trickery with graphics

A great trick that makes an increase look even more impressive is to use pictograms to misrepresent statistics. In his book *How to Lie with Statistics*, Darrell Huff gives an example of this. He points out a useful way to make American weekly wages appear better than twice those of people in a mythical country he called Rotund. He begins by drawing a moneybag to represent the $325 weekly wage of someone in Rotund, then he draws another one twice as tall to represent the American's $750 weekly wage. Huff explains: '*That's in proportion, isn't it? The American's wage appears to dwarf the foreigner's. What a great place to live! The catch, of course, is this: while the second bag is twice as high as the first, it is also twice as wide. It occupies not twice but four times as much area on the page. The numbers will still say that wage difference is two to one, but the visual impression, which is the dominating one most of the time, says the ratio is four to one.*'

The diagram below shows how this trick works. Let's imagine that Business A employs a certain number of staff and Business B employs three times as many. The properly scaled pictogram on the left shows this relationship accurately. However, Business B wants to make its employment statistics look even more impressive, so it chooses to use improper scaling to achieve this effect (middle graph). The diagram on the right shows why the middle graph is misleading, visually overstating the true situation.

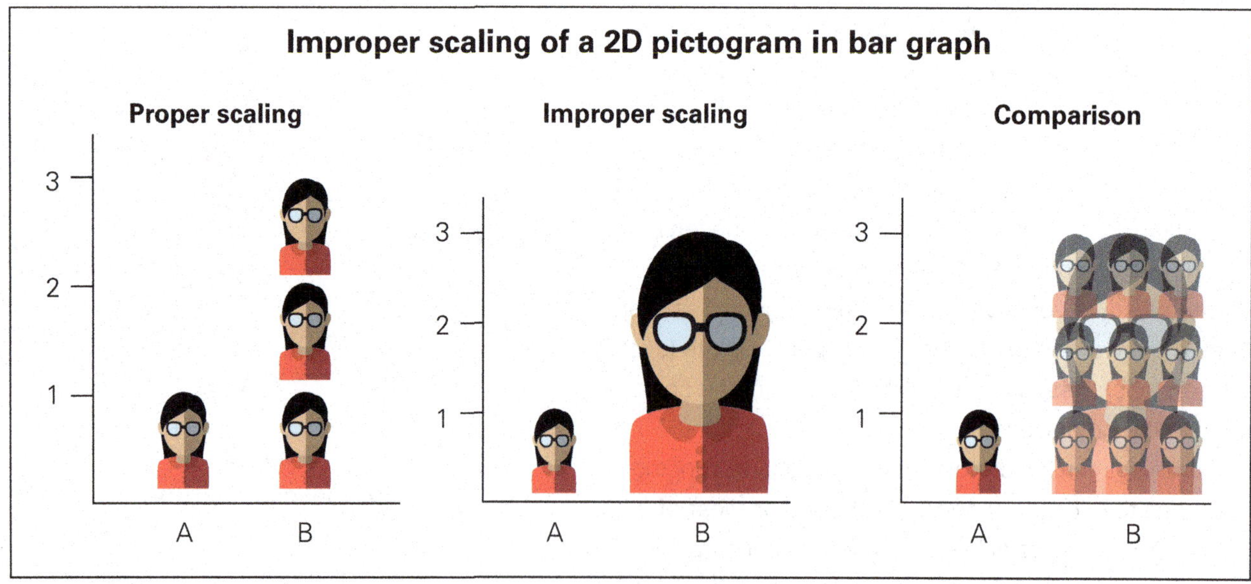

ISBN: 9780170418393

Trickery with trends

When two or more lines appear together in a graph – and they look similar to each other – we tend to assume that they are related. The red line in this chart represents deaths from drug overdoses in the United States, while the green line represents spending on science and technology – two completely unrelated sets of data.

At first glance, however, it appears that as the US spends more on science, an increasing number of people are dying from drug overdoses. Using this graph, it might be possible for someone involved with drug addiction treatment to claim that their service is being starved of funding because of the increased spending on science. Conversely, it could be argued that as overdose deaths increase, the US feels it needs to spend more on technology!

There is, of course, no direct connection between these two items. Perceptual scientist Ruth Rosenholtz points out that we like trends because they tell a story that makes data more meaningful; that's why we're always on the lookout for connections even when they don't exist. In statistics, rejection of this false relationship is summed up by the statement that 'correlation does not imply causation'.

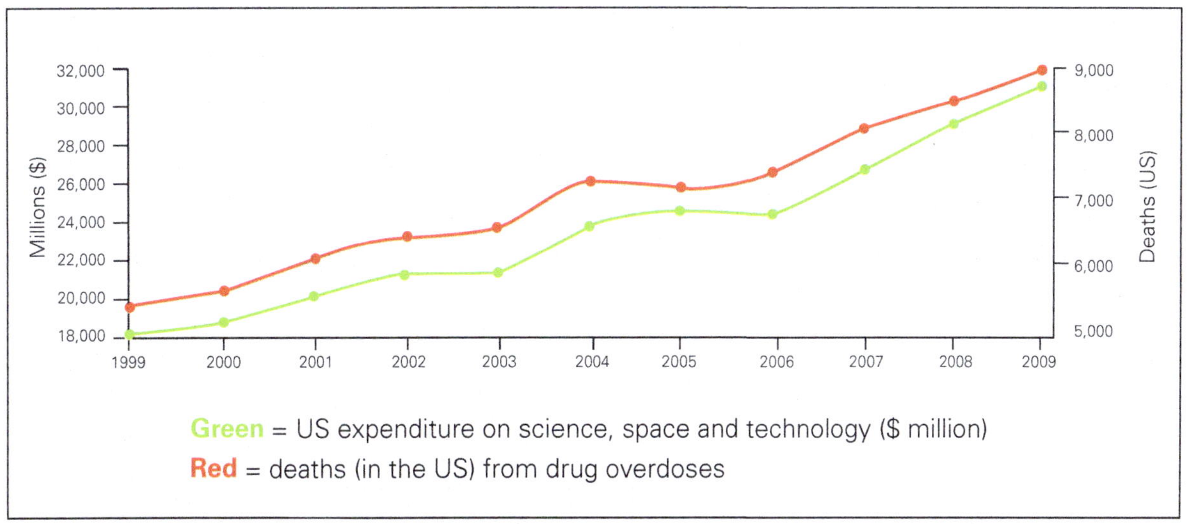

Trickery with TMI (too much information)

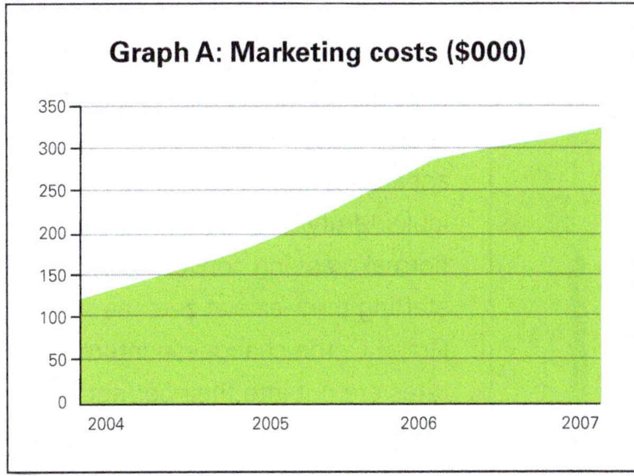

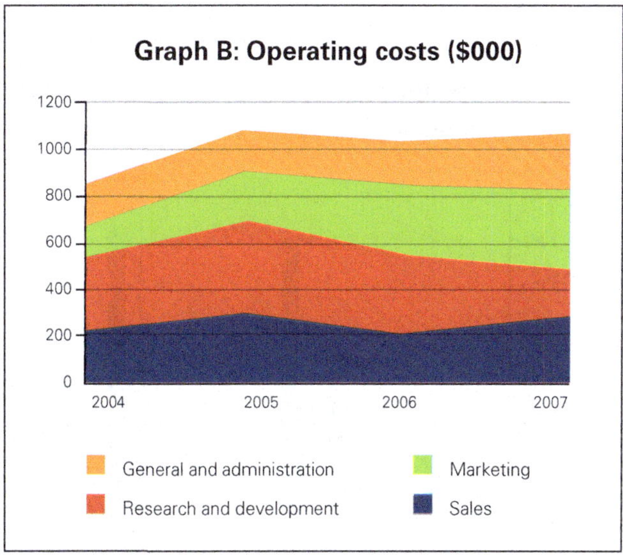

Analysing statistics, graphs and maps

ISBN: 9780170418393

The marketing team in this company is embarrassed that their expenditure has increased almost three-fold over four years. Income from sales, however, has not increased nearly as much. What to do? Graph A shows this expenditure all too readily, so why not 'hide' the data in plain sight among other expenditure data? Graph B shows the same three-fold increase in marketing expenditure, but now its impact is softened by the inclusion of other data not relevant to what's going on in marketing. Problem solved!

'Comparing the change in height between data sets while they also move up and down is not a natural visual task for us,' says Rosenholtz. *'It's not clear to me whether I'm supposed to be looking at the overall height or the width or what. Any kind of comparison like that is more cognitive [requiring careful thought] ...'*

Trickery with a change of scale

At first glance the two graphs below seem to show two sets of unrelated data; however, a closer look reveals that the only difference is the scale. In Graph A, the manager of the sales team feels that the results don't look good enough. What to do? While Graph A starts as it should at zero, the manager has decided in Graph B that by zooming in closer, the results – after a dip – will look stunning. This is especially so when the sales for December (the month is omitted for greater effect) go 'off the chart'!

This trick works because it's difficult for us to examine a chart's scale and data at the same time, says Rosenholtz. Instead, we take on board the general trend first then, if we're critical consumers of information, we look more closely at the scale. By that point, though, our first impression has already been made.

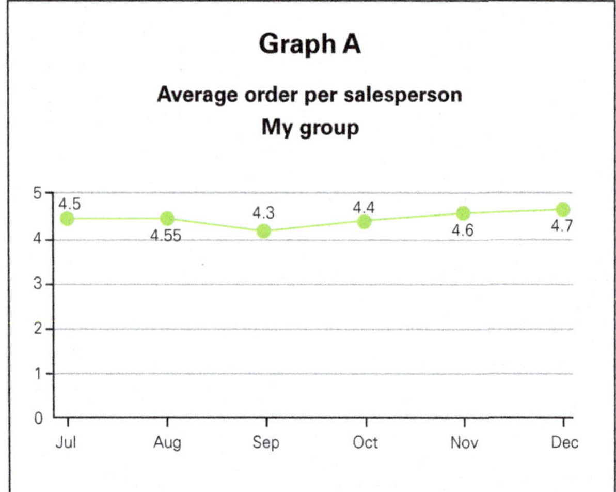

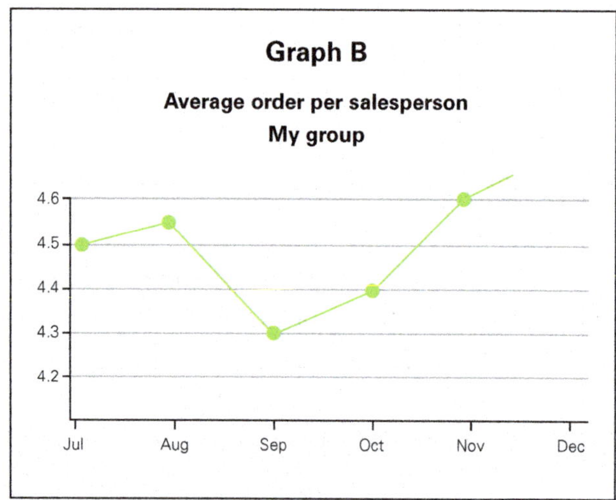

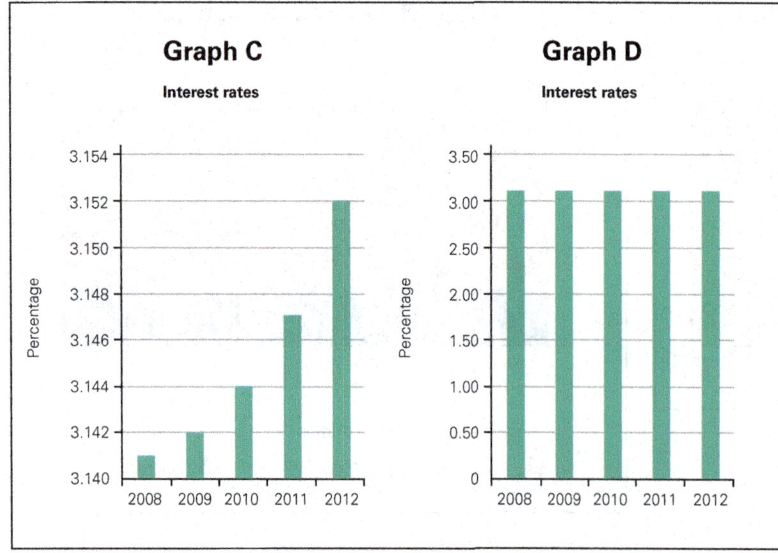

Here's another version of the same attempt at trickery. The *y*-axis in Graph C does not start at zero; the apparently rapid rise in interest rates looks terrifying! However, using normal graphing conventions and starting the *y*-axis at zero, as per Graph D, the changes in interest rates are put into their correct context.

ISBN: 9780170418393

Another example. In 2005, Terry Schiavo was removed from life support in the US after a years-long court battle. The TV news channel CNN used a graph similar to the one here to show who (based on political affiliation) agreed with the decision to remove the feeding tube.

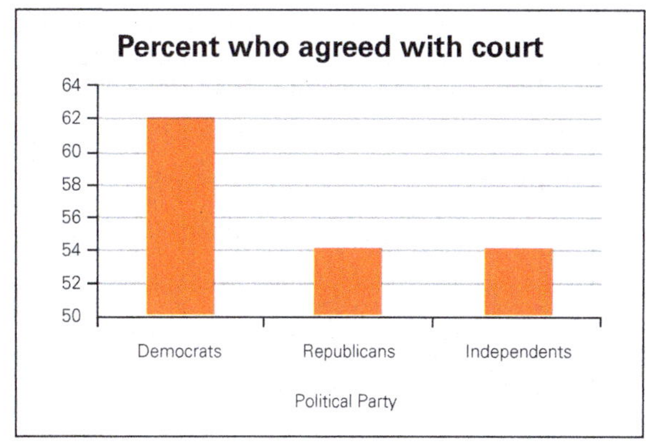

At first glance it looks like three times as many Democrats supported the decision; however, closer inspection reveals that the *y*-axis scale does not start at zero. In reality, only eight percentage points separate the two parties: Democrats supported the decision only a little more than Republicans.

Below is another version of the same trick of changing the scale on either axis to achieve a desired effect. If the goal is to make the change look dramatic, reduce the *x*-axis scale and increase the *y*-axis scale (stretch the graph upwards) as in the middle graph; conversely, the change can be made to look much more limited by compressing the graph, as in the right-hand one.

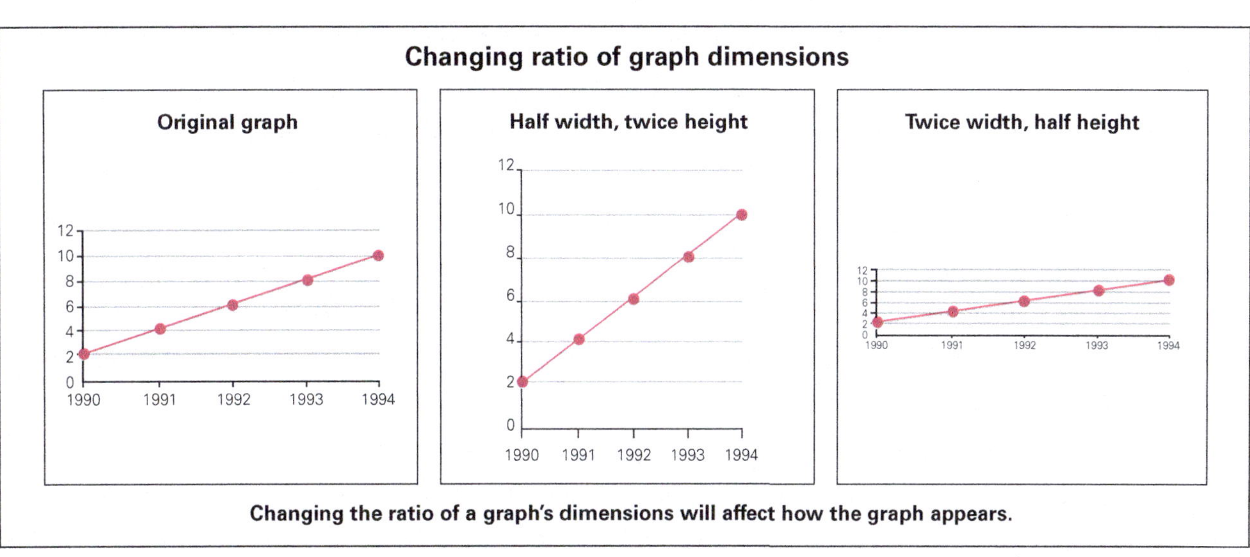

Changing the ratio of a graph's dimensions will affect how the graph appears.

Trickery with a double *y*-axis

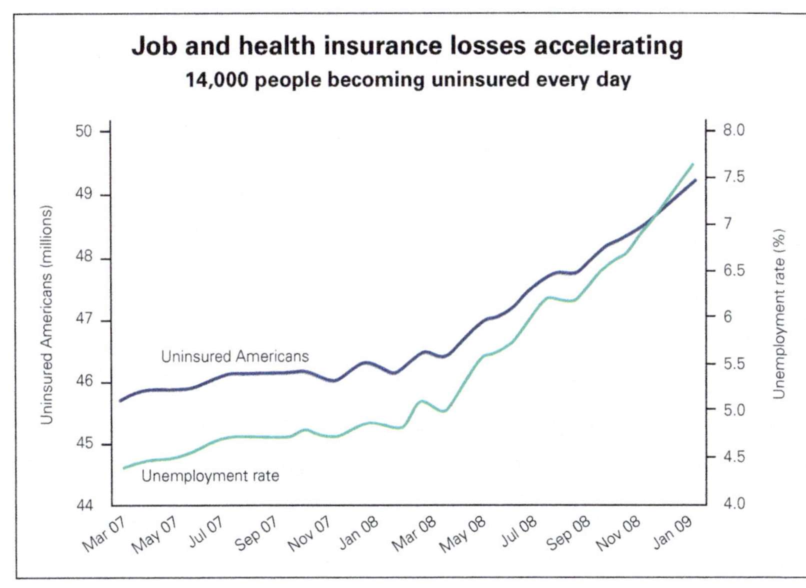

At first glance, it looks clear that job and health insurance losses are indeed accelerating and, it seems fair enough to say, this is a bad thing. However, a closer look at the graph reveals that there are two *y*-axes. This special type of trickery puts two different sets of data, with different scales, on the same graph, once again making it look as though there is a clear connection between the two. (There may actually be, but this is not the right or truthful way to show it.) Beware the double *y*-axis!

ISBN: 9780170418393

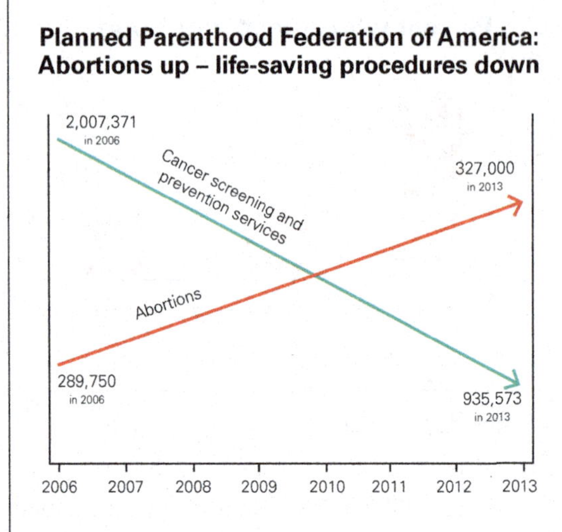

From online magazine *Quartz* comes this analysis of falsification of a presentation by opponents of Planned Parenthood, a women's health group in America that includes abortions as part of its services to women. Republican opponents claimed in 2015 that federal funding was being used to support an increase in abortions, while other more valuable services were being ignored. A graph with a double *y*-axis with no scale for either was produced as 'evidence'. Congressman Jason Chaffetz of Utah explained the chart: 'In blue, that's the reduction in breast exams, and the red is the increase in the abortions. That's what's going on in your organization [Planned Parenthood].'

At first glance (notice how many times that expression has been used in this section), it indeed appears that Planned Parenthood have effectively become an abortion service. Perhaps it would be right to cut federal funding if it was indeed neglecting its other responsibilities. However, this graph has real problems. Visually it appears that 327,000 (the number of abortions) is a larger number than 935,573 (the number of cancer prevention services).

Here's how the graph should have looked, if presented according to the usual conventions. It is true that the number of screening services has declined, but there might be a range of explanations for this. What is clear, and is a contradiction of the congressman's assertions, is that abortions are not dramatically increasing.

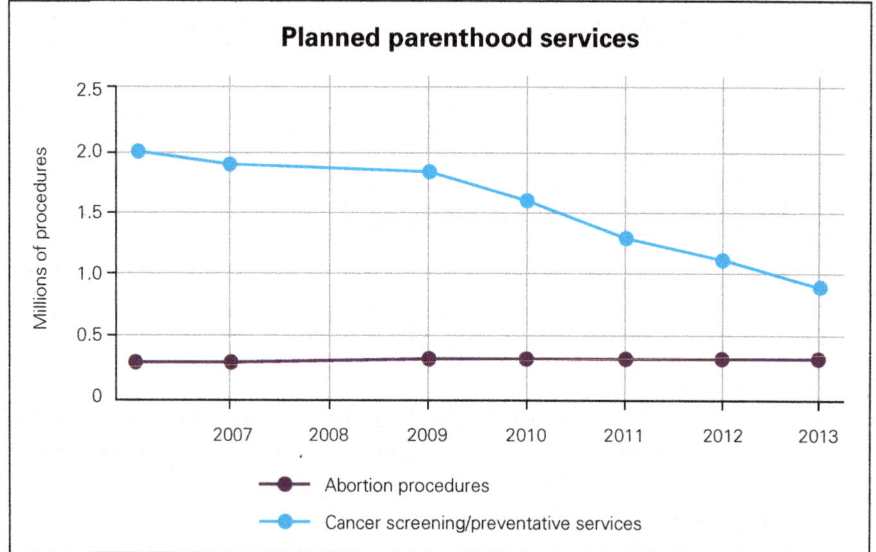

 ISBN: 9780170418393

12 Analysing maps

While at first glance maps might seem as uncomplicated and inherently reliable as graphs and statistics did initially, the same sort of cautions apply and the same sort of questions must be asked of them. Maps are created by people, and because of this, bias and misrepresentation, whether deliberate or not, can creep in. When thinking about who is making the map (or paying for it to be made), you can use many of the same 'CAP' analysis questions with which you analyse a primary source (see pages 36–37).

It is important to keep in mind that a map is created for a **purpose**. It might be to show where the continents and oceans are, or railways and roads, or tramping tracks or locations of medical centres. Maps can show population densities, wealth distribution or climate conditions. In fact, there is an almost limitless number of things that maps can show. Clearly, decisions are made by the map-maker on what to include and what to exclude. While this makes perfect sense, such choices can bring in bias, whether intentional or not. Furthermore, what individual map-makers and societies find 'interesting', 'important' and worthy of study changes over time. It is also influenced by many factors, including political, social and economic beliefs and values. For example, there is not much reason today to produce maps of whaling stations in New Zealand, but up to the mid-1800s, such maps had real economic value. In the United States in the 1890s, it was easy to find atlases and maps of voting patterns, wineries, railroads and rivers, but not a single map on the status of women. When analysing historical maps we need to explore, where possible, beyond the map itself in order to fully interpret it.

World maps: Caution!

There are some significant issues with one of the most common maps we use: the map of the earth's surface. To make a two-dimensional map from a spherical globe, cartographers *(map-makers)* have to *project* the spherical surface onto a two-dimensional piece of paper (or computer screen). This is not as easy as it might sound.

There are around *70* different valid ways of doing these 'projections'. Each of them has an impact on the way we see the world. The problem is that to produce the usual rectangular maps we use, map-makers have to deform the spherical surface of the earth by stretching it and/or compressing it somewhere. The nature of these compressions and stretches will determine what the continents and oceans look like in relation to each other. Because there is no one way that works perfectly everywhere on a two-dimensional map, all of them are inaccurate in some way. The trick is to find one that has the least errors for your purpose. On the other hand, those who wish to deceive or influence others can also choose a particular projection that suits their purposes.

ISBN: 9780170418393

A 'flat-Earth' map drawn by Orlando Ferguson in 1893. The main text explains: 'Four Hundred Passages in the Bible that Condemns the Globe Theory, or the Flying Earth, and None Sustain It. This Map is the Bible Map of the World.'

Map-making background

Mercator projection

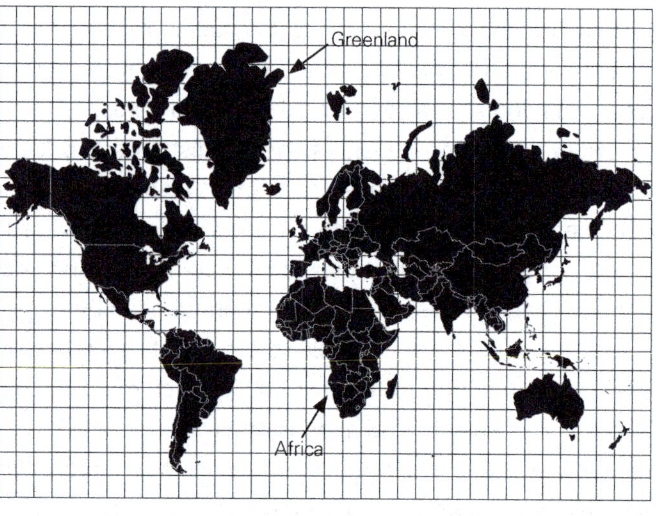

The earliest maps in Greece, Rome, China, Persia and the Islamic world were created without much reference to the mathematics needed to accurately portray a sphere on a flat surface. Then, in 1569, the Flemish geographer and cartographer Gerardus Mercator for the first time used a mathematical formula to represent latitude and longitude on a map. His formula – called the Mercator projection – quickly became popular among navigators because the directions of the compass – north, east, south and west – matched those on the map. While it didn't matter too much for navigational purposes, the Mercator projection distorted areas and distances at the top and bottom of the map; the North and South Poles extend unrealistically. Similarly, land masses to the far north and south appear much larger than they actually are, while those nearer the equator seem smaller by comparison. For example, on the Mercator projection shown here, Greenland appears to be larger than Africa. In fact, Africa is 14 times bigger in area than Greenland! However, as Europe began to dominate the globe and global trade from around the time of Mercator's map, it suited those in power that Europe's size was exaggerated. This fitted with their view of its dominant place in the world.

In contrast, the Goode homolosine projection, developed in 1923 to overcome some of the key problems with the Mercator projection, keeps the land areas of the continents in proportion (although not perfectly). However, while the version shown here has just four lobes, normally this type of map is presented with many more. For most ordinary users the shape of this map is not very useful. The simpler and politically more satisfying Mercator projection thus persisted mostly unchallenged in popular world maps until at least the mid-20th century.

Goode homolosine projection

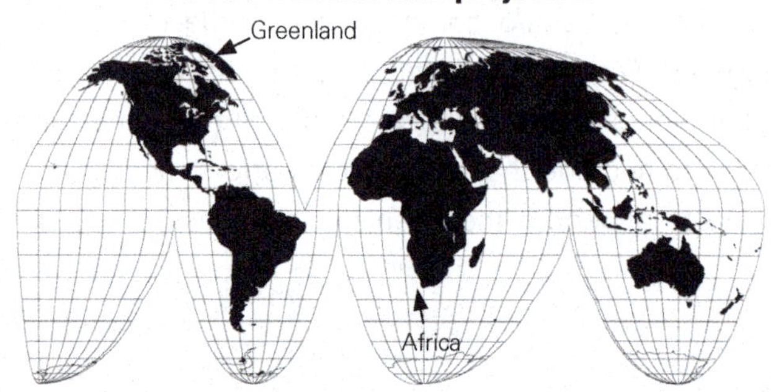

 ISBN: 9780170418393

Politics and maps

Maps can be used for political purposes. The standard Mercator projection is used in Map A; the countries coloured red are the communist Warsaw Pact nations during the Cold War. (The Cold War was the nuclear-armed rivalry between the two world superpowers after World War II, communist Russia and capitalist USA.) To the immediate west of the 'red menace' are the nations of Western Europe, key American allies.

Map A: Mercator projection

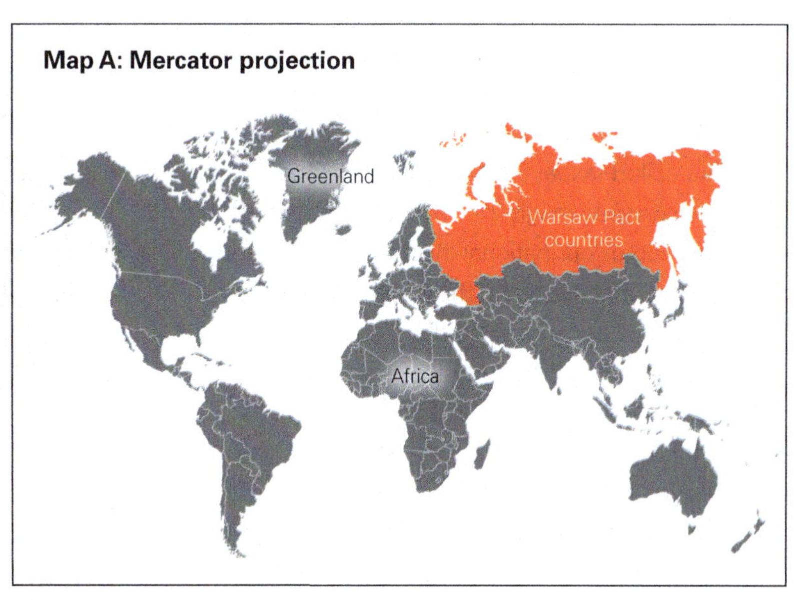

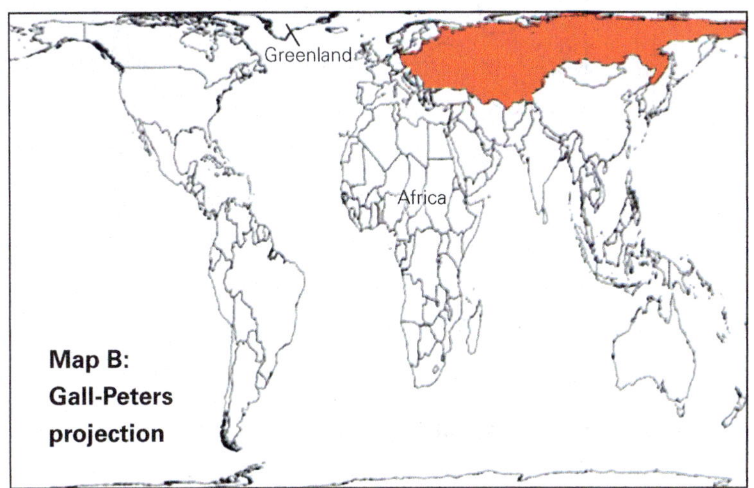

Map B: Gall-Peters projection

In Map B, the Gall-Peters projection is used. All land areas are shown the correct sizes relative to each other. For example, Africa does indeed look 14 times bigger than Greenland, as it is. This is not true for the Mercator projection (Map A). Furthermore Russia and its eastern European allies no longer look quite so menacing.

If, as the American government, you believed it important to convince the American people that military spending needed to be increased, the polar projection (opposite) would help communicate the idea of a vast 'red menace' more so than the Gall-Peters map.

Polar projection

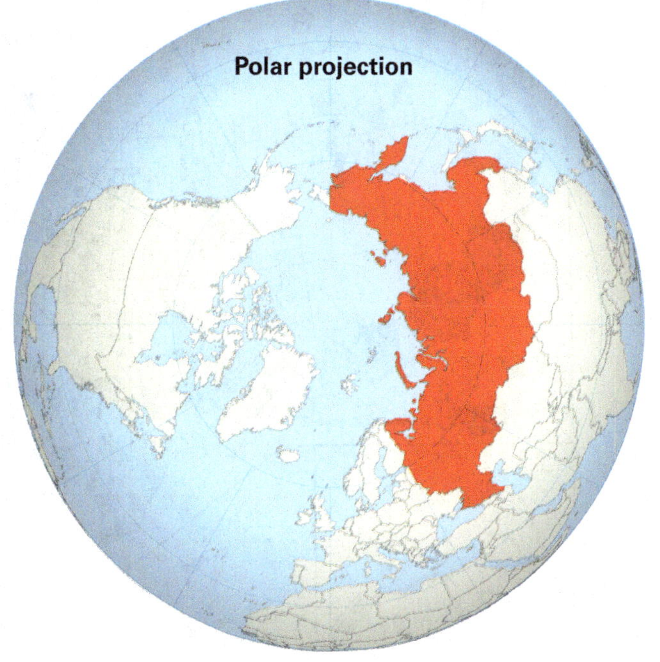

ISBN: 9780170418393

This next attempt at graphic trickery comes straight from Darrell Huff's book *How to Lie with Statistics*, so I'll let him tell the story.

> 'The Darkening Shadow' graphic was published in the 1950s by the First National Bank of Boston (USA) and was reproduced widely by so-called taxpayers groups, newspapers, and *Newsweek* magazine. The map shows what portion of our national income is now being taken, and spent, by the federal government. It does this by shading the areas of the states west of the Mississippi (excepting only Louisiana, Arkansas, and part of Missouri) to indicate that federal spending has become equal to the total incomes of the people of those states. It looks bad! The deception lies in choosing states having large land areas but, because of sparse *[thin]* population, relatively small incomes. With equal honesty (and equal dishonesty) the map maker might have started shading in New York or New England and come out with a vastly smaller and less impressive shadow. Using the same data he would have produced quite a different impression in the mind of anyone who looked at his map.

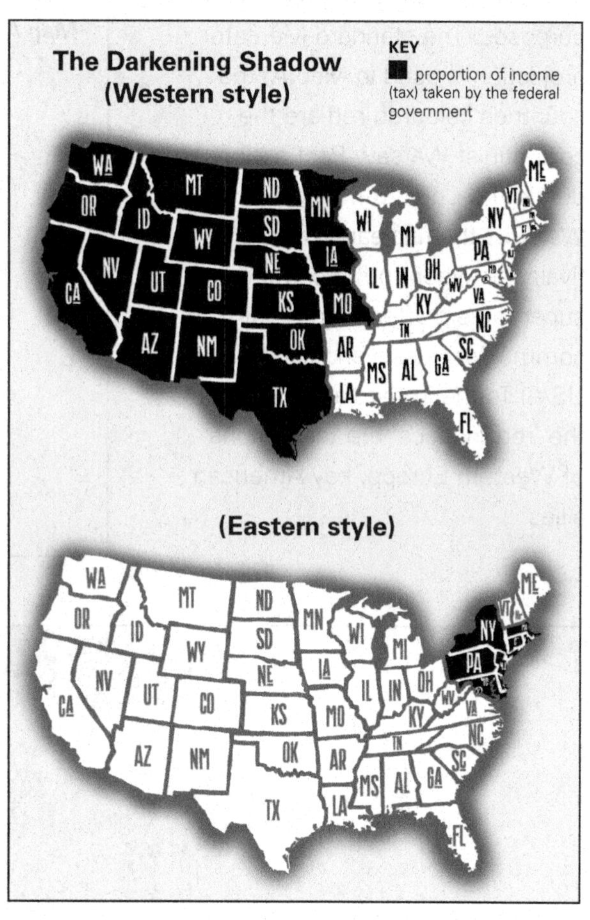

Compare the two maps above to the Population Density map below. The darkest areas are the most densely populated.

Population density, by counties, 1960

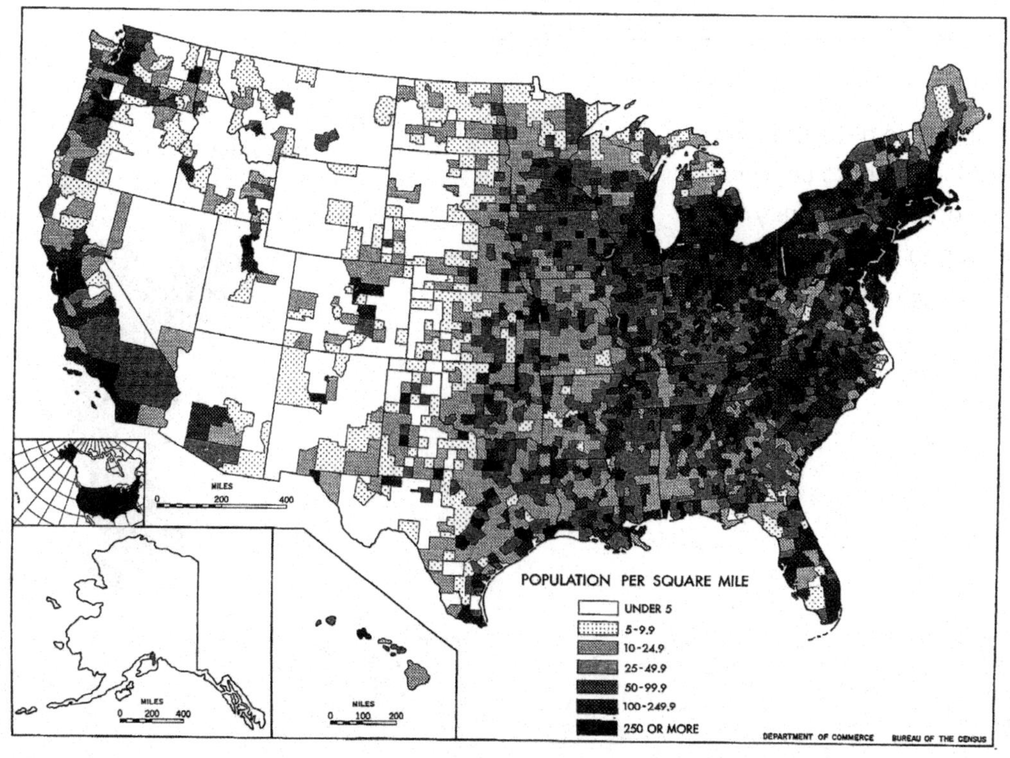

 ISBN: 9780170418393

Tools for analysing a map

While the 'CAP' source analysis tools (see pages 36–37) are also very useful for analysing maps, here are some more map-specific questions you can use to guide your thinking. Refer also to the exemplar that follows.

Questions to ask of a map

1 What information can we find in the map? Where applicable, consider:
- title, scale, key, date of production
- features shown in the map, including any labels. What appears to be most prominent/significant?

2 Who made the map, and for what purpose? Is there any bias, intentional or not?

3 How was the map created? What source of information was used?

4 What is missing from the map that you might have expected to see?

5 What other sorts of information would you want to find in order to confirm your analysis of this map?

Be sure to ask any of your own questions, too, and feel free to speculate briefly on what the answers might be!

Map analysis exemplar

Village of Rijswijk, Netherlands (Holland), probably 16th century

ISBN: 9780170418393

Possible questions

While your responses do not need to be as full as this, you should try to extract all you can from the map.

1 As the title says, this is a village (Rijswijk) in Holland in the 1500s. There is no scale or key. This may be because map rules didn't exist back then, or were different. In the map, three main roads extending from the centre of town are shown, one each going west, east and south (there are also two smaller ones on the eastern side). Are they connected to other villages/towns? They seem big enough to take a horse and cart, so goods might be transported on them. The largest building appears to be a (Christian) church; there are also about 30–40 other houses (are there also workshops such as blacksmiths?) along the main streets. Away from the main centre there are scattered houses, along with fields that are fenced. There are quite a few trees as well. There is a stream (or is it another road?) coming in from the northeast corner; this could be the village water supply. There is some writing on the map but it is too small to read. The map is in colour; is this significant?

2 We have no information on who made the map but presumably they were Dutch and literate (the writing on the map). Presumably the purpose was just to show the layout of the village and its size? In terms of bias, maybe the church is shown over-large to emphasise its status?

3 Presumably the map-maker either lived in the village (maybe part of the church?) or visited, perhaps as part of an official survey? The land seems very flat so there might not have been a hill to look down on the village. This would mean creating the map from walking around it.

4 It's hard to tell if there are any animals; maybe they just grow crops in this village. There doesn't seem to be a really big house such as the 'Lord of the Manor' might have ... There doesn't seem to be any sort of fortification, so either this is unrealistic or there is no need for it.

5 Church records (births, deaths, marriages) and any other official documents. Letters or diaries from any of the villagers, if this is realistic. A list of the 'businesses' in the village. A map showing the surrounding areas.

ISBN: 9780170418393

1 ACTIVITY

Use the five 'Questions to ask of a map' on page 117 as a guide to help your analysis of the maps below. When completed, share your analysis with the rest of the class.

Map 1

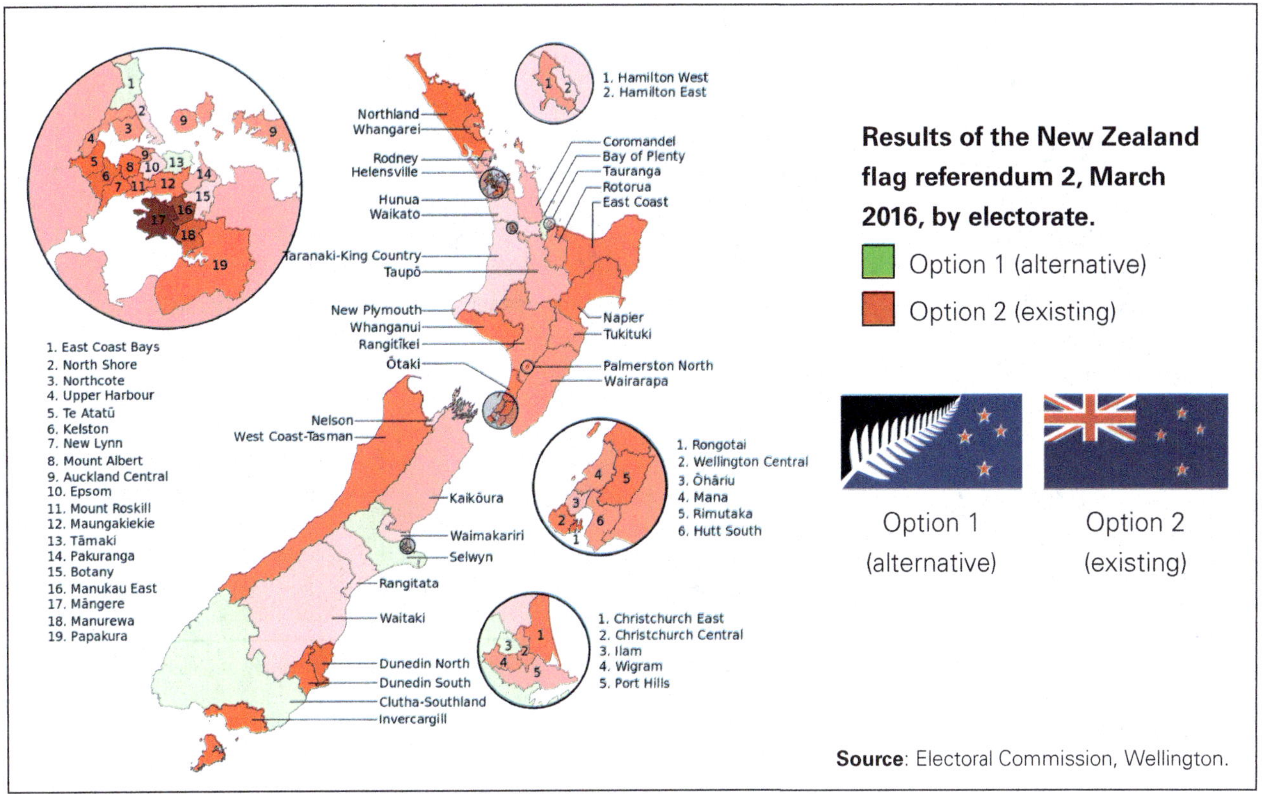

Map 1 analysis: ______________________________

____

____

____

____

____

____

____

____

____

____

____

- Discuss your response with others in the class.

ISBN: 9780170418393

Map 2

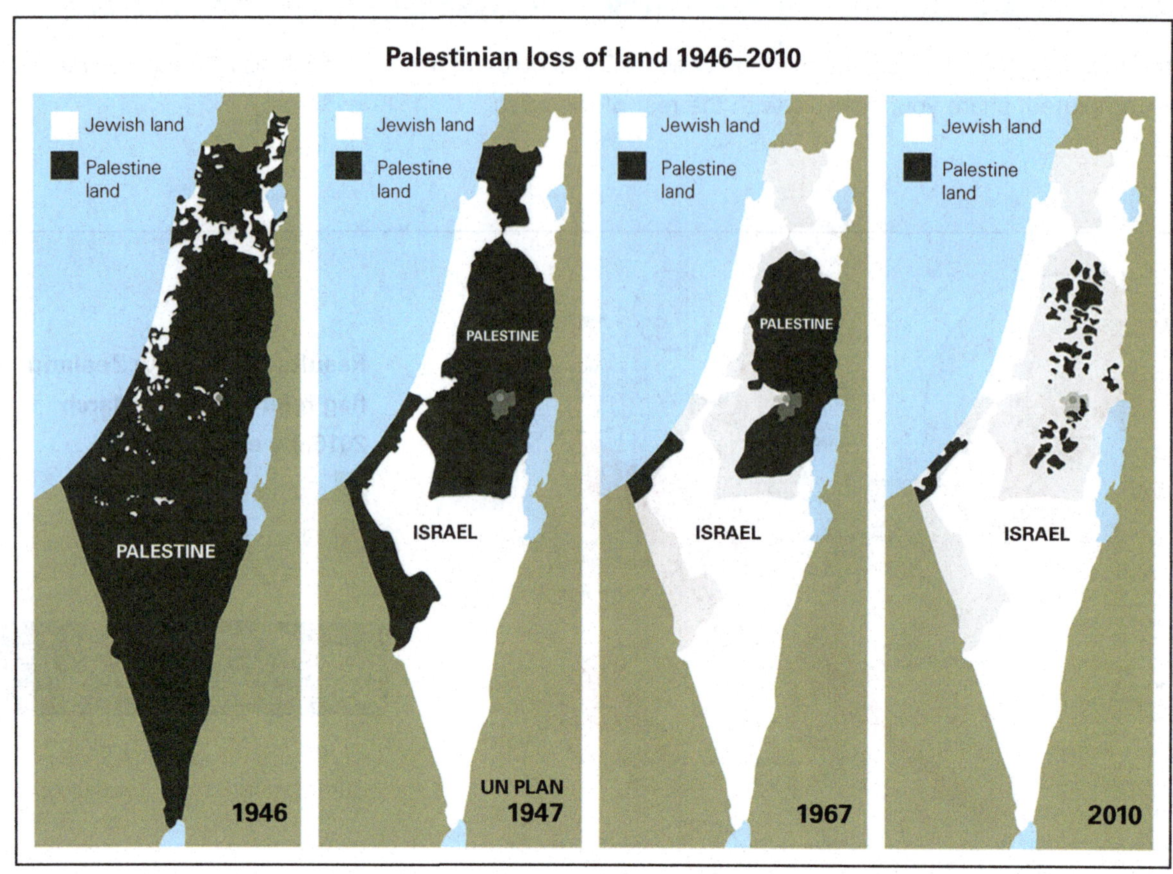

Source: *Journal of World Literature Today,* University of Oklahoma, 2012.

Map 2 analysis: ______________________________

____

____

____

____

____

____

____

____

____

____

____

____

- Discuss your response with others in the class.

 ISBN: 9780170418393

Map 3

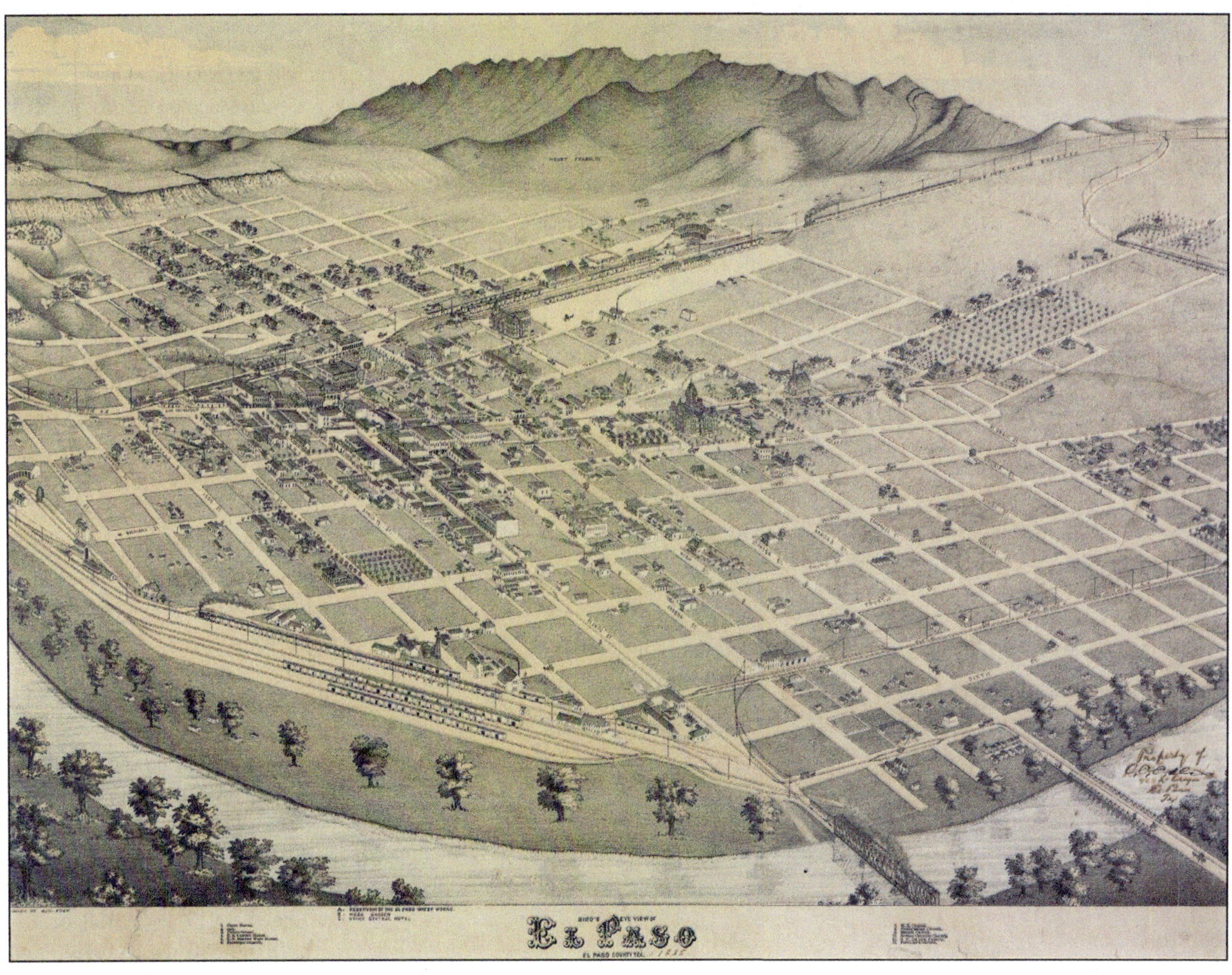

Bird's-eye view of El Paso, Texas, 1886.

Source: Augustus Koch, map-maker, 1886.

Map 3 analysis:

- Discuss your response with others in the class.

ISBN: 9780170418393

Map 4

Migration arrows are supported by the following sources.

From Taiwan through Melanesia to Polynesia, and earlier migration to Australia and New Guinea:

- Yoshan Moodley, Bodo Linz, Yoshio Yamaoka, Helen M. Windsor, Sebastien Breurec, Jeng-Yih Wu, Ayas Maady, Steffie Bernhöft, Jean-Michel Thiberge, Suparat Phuanukoonnon, Gangolf Jobb, Peter Siba, David Y. Graham, Barry J. Marshall, and Mark Achtman (2009). 'The Peopling of the Pacific from a Bacterial Perspective', *Science*, 23 January 2009: 323 (5913), 527–530. doi:10.1126/science.1166083

Colonisation of East Polynesia, and dispersal to more remote islands (including Hawaii, Easter Island, and New Zealand):

- Janet M. Wilmshurst, Terry L. Hunt, Carl P. Lipo, and Atholl J. Anderson (2011). 'High-precision radiocarbon dating shows recent and rapid initial human colonization of East Polynesia', Proceedings of the National Academy of Sciences of the United States of America, 1 February 2011, vol. 108, no. 5, 1815–1820. doi:10.1073/pnas.1015876108

Map 4 analysis: ______________________________

____

____

____

____

____

____

____

____

____

____

____

____

- Discuss your response with others in the class.

ISBN: 9780170418393

Map 5

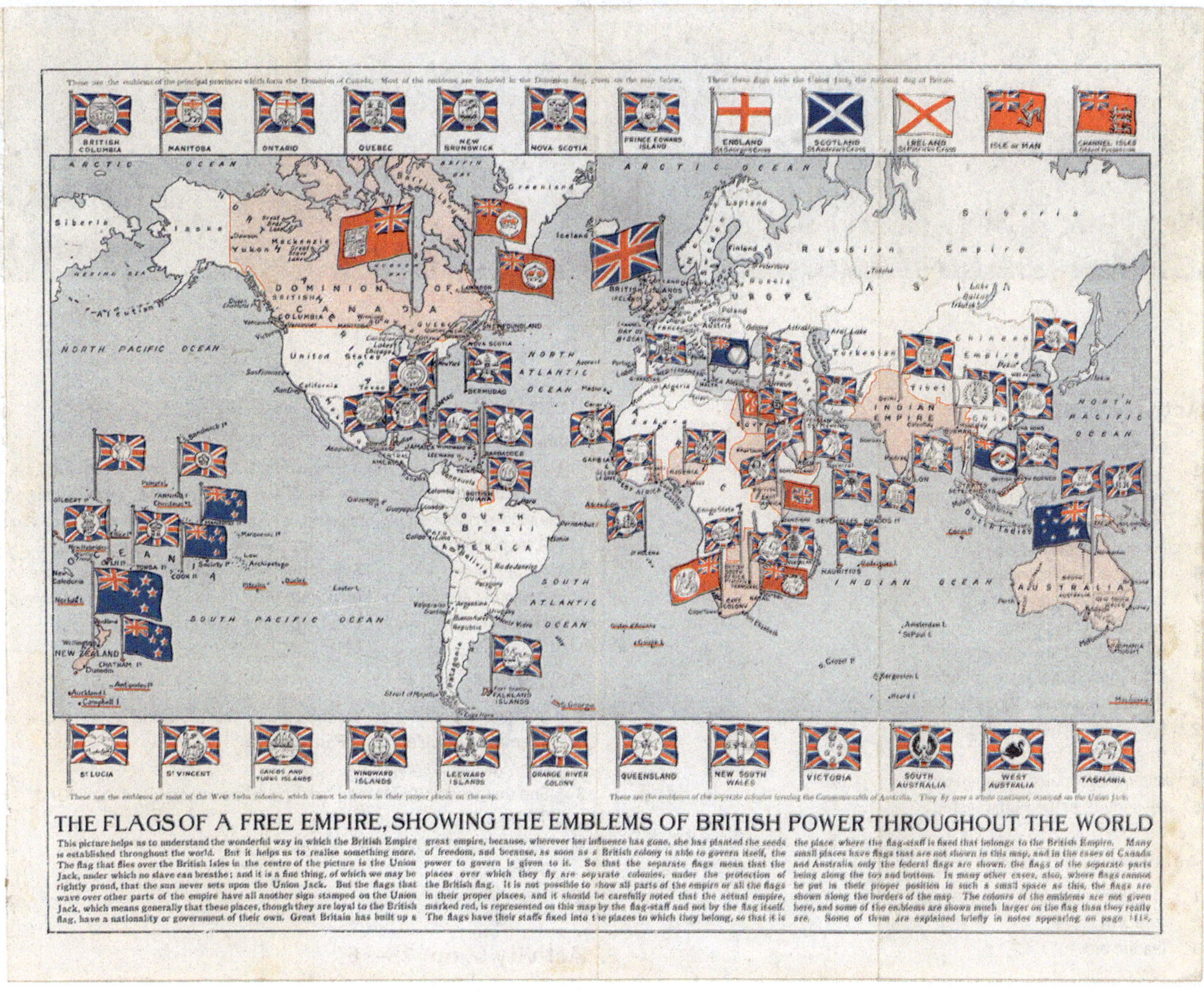

British Empire, 1910 (produced by the British government).

Map 5 analysis: ____

- Discuss your response with others in the class.

ISBN: 9780170418393

Answers

Activity 1, pp. 4–5

1 hostility; extreme dislike
2 related to the eye
3 high praise (the definition is right in the sentence)
4 rejection; refutation; negation
5 insanity; madness; lunacy
6 thin; spare; light; meagre
7 religious; sincere; devout
8 hatred; loathing; disgust
9 reprove; caution; reprimand; tell off
10 followers; students; learners
11 excessive; surplus; unnecessary
12 disloyal; treacherous; deceitful
13 trite; clichéd; worn out; overused
14 showy; pompous; exaggerated
15 respected; esteemed; revered

Activity 2, pp. 5–6

1 changes/reforms/improvements, etc.
2 freedom
3 leader, etc.
4 responsible, etc.
5 educate/teach/inform/instruct, etc.
6 principles/ideas/beliefs, etc.
7 extended/given/granted, etc., and classified/grouped/lumped together, etc.
8 petitions and petition
9 congratulating
10 election, and exercised/were granted, etc.

Activity 1, pp. 8–9

Skimming: text summary

At first, most of the Pakeha women in New Zealand were the wives of Christian missionaries. After the Treaty in 1840 came an increasing number of settlers and their 'pioneer wives'. For most of the growing number of British women, in the 1860s and 1870s, marriage was still the 'main occupation'. As New Zealand was transformed from a Maori country to a settler colony by the late 19th century, middle class women began to focus on social issues.

Activity 2, p. 10

1 Describes the importance of women's roles on mission stations: holding things together, especially while the men were away.
2 The isolated nature of the frontier society brought with it problems for women such as loneliness, male alcoholism and violence, diseases, and problems with childbirth.
3 The percentage of women who were single according to the 1874 census: marriage was the main female 'occupation'.
4 In Judith Malone's words, women were inferior in the eyes of the law in areas such as divorce, pay rates, property, education, morality and political and social rights.

Activity 3, pp. 10–13

Skimming: text summary

The women who led the fight for women's suffrage were determined, strong-minded, committed to the cause and articulate in their arguments. These women include Kate Sheppard, who is the most well-known; Ada Wells fought for equality for women; Margaret Sievwright was shy but worked hard for the cause; Amey Daldy was much stroppier and Lady Stout was also strong-minded, fearless and outspoken; Marion Hatton only became involved in her late fifties; Annie Schnackenberg was a leading feminist.

Activity 4, p. 14

1 Suffrage opponents coined the phrase 'The Shrieking Sisterhood' in an attempt to ridicule them. (Paragraph 1)
2 Ada Wells. (Paragraph 3)
3 She resigned as Auckland Franchise Superintendent of the WCTU. (Paragraph 5)
4 Securing education for all women irrespective of race or class. (Paragraph 6)
5 1864. (Paragraph 8)

Activity 5, pp. 15–16

1 able to express points clearly
2 allotted/appointed
3 scorn/ridicule
4 nickname/label
5 identical/the same as
6 support/back
7 empowerment/suffrage/vote
8 knowledge/understanding
9 representative/delegate
10 relax/'take it easy'
11 involved/entangled
12 supervised/headed
13 initial/introductory
14 law/regulation

Activity 3, pp. 21–29

Event 1a – Task 1: Vocabulary

1 in war, the killed and wounded
2 first time/never experienced before
3 military equipment and supplies
4 The interaction between geography (places) and political power; in this case it was changes of borders and systems of political authority (collapse of empires).
5 aggravating/continuing to annoy

Event 1b – Task 2: Vocabulary

1 main fighting groups/people/countries
2 made up of
3 non-fighters/civilians
4 occupation and control of other countries, willingly or unwillingly, by European powers
5 in small steps/amounts

ISBN: 9780170418393

Event 2a – Task 1: Vocabulary
1 rulership by a family, over generations
2 passionately/deeply
3 workable/practical/feasible
4 set of political beliefs/ideas
5 safeguard/protection/barrier
6 without directly saying so

EVENT 2b – Task 2: Vocabulary
1 invented/devised
2 possibility/probability
3 excess/surplus
4 where the main powers do not directly fight each other but support opposing sides in a conflict
5 put at risk/endanger
6 workable/practical/viable

EVENT 3a – Task 1: Vocabulary
1 in a range of different places
2 strip/band
3 to make unable to function optimally (at peak performance)
4 refugees/those who have been banished
5 full political authority
6 unrestricted/unimpeded

EVENT 3b – Task 2: Vocabulary
1 almost totally destroyed
2 independence/self-rule
3 conform/take on the ways of a different culture
4 contested/argued
5 those seeking to buy up land cheaply and on-sell it at a profit, rather than keep and use it
6 wicked/destructive

EVENT 3c – Task 4: Vocabulary
1 stop/cease
2 groups/factions
3 use freely/carry out
4 side-lined/downgraded
5 criticising/calling to account
6 sense of duty/obligation, rather than having to do something

Activity 1, pp. 38–40

1 Primary. Although it was created a long time after the event described, Alfons Heck did witness the event himself.
2 **Points to consider could include**: the effects of memory nearly fifty years after the event, although Heck's post-war discussions with his professor suggest he didn't just 'forget' this period until writing his book. Being a book it is a public document so he might want to appear 'more innocent' than he was (although he was just a child at the time). The book could also be an attempt to make money so he *might* embellish things. However, other sources will probably support Heck's version of the past and, taken with these, one could probably judge this to be reasonably reliable.
3 Overall we get a sense of what it was like to be a young person (of the right racial background) in Germany at this time. Examples for the specific paragraphs could be (but are not limited to):
   a Hitler knew how to 'play' the crowd well. The rally was clearly organised ('...as we had been instructed') rather than spontaneous. What would crowds have been like if it wasn't organised?
   b The 'personal touch' in Hitler's speech seems to have had an impact, helping him identify with the crowd. According to Hitler, class divisions no longer existed in Germany – an idea worth exploring more.
   c Hitler clearly believed that getting the youth onside was important. Personal connection was too: '...with his eyes seemingly fixed on me...' shows the power of Hitler's oratory.
   d At least some former Nazis (the professor) seem to have done well after the war. The self-belief in Hitler's time of Germany's right to rule seems to have been widespread.

4 Other young people's views in diaries, letters or interviews; German (and foreign) newspaper reports of the time; official Nazi reports and/or diaries of leading Nazis etc.
5 The key issue is the 'adoration' shown and responses could discuss this.

Activity 2, pp. 41–42

1 Very reliable. It is an official communication from one SS official to a superior. It was also presented as evidence to the post-war Trials of War Criminals. A possible limitation *might* be that as it is a report to a superior officer the author might want to make himself look 'good' in it.
2 Other medical/official reports; the response (if any) from Himmler; other evidence supplied to the Nuremburg Trials; accounts of any surviving concentration camp inmates etc. (There will likely be no newspaper reports from the time, given the nature of this 'research'.)

Activity 3, pp. 43–44

1 Quite reliable? It appears to be the words of a slave telling of his own experiences. However, it's hard to know who actually typed it up (presumably a slave could not type or have access to a typewriter?) or how the interview was conducted. Would Mingo feel comfortable revealing the truth to his interviewer? His words do seem to have been taken down as actually spoken and he does talk openly about the threat of beatings. In the excerpt we have he does seem to be remembering back to his childhood – memory issues?
2 Other slaves' accounts (especially if this account was part of an organised attempt to record slaves' experiences). Newspaper reports, including slave sale notices. Slave owners' accounts, from interviews (if any), letters, diaries etc.

Activity 3, pp. 66–69

Possible answers
If your responses differ, discuss them with the class/your teacher.

Short-term
- Wakefield Company's plans and arrival of the *Tory*. British concerns re republics being set up.
- Strength/influence of the humanitarian movement.
- French immigrant ship on its way to Akaroa?

Long-term
- Lawlessness, e.g. the *Elizabeth* incident.
- 1831 call by chiefs for Britain to do something about lawlessness and subsequent ineffectiveness of Busby.
- Investor pressure. (Or is this short-term?)
- Earlier arrival of sealers, whalers and traders, attracted by Cook's reports?
- Increasing French presence?

Underlying
- British sense of superiority and 'destiny' to 'civilise' the 'unenlightened'.
- British voyages of exploration, bringing Europe to New Zealand.
- Traditional rivalries of Britain and France.

Activity 4, pp. 70–73

Possible answers
If your responses differ, discuss them with the class/your teacher.

Short-term
- Growing arrogance and disrespect of Pakeha traders.
- The 'solemn bond' implied between Crown and Maori.
- Role of the missionaries in persuading Maori.
- Rangatiratanga guaranteed, especially as Maori were dominant in all ways in New Zealand in 1840.

Long-term

- Lawlessness and ineffectiveness of Busby. (Or is this short-term?)
- Enthusiasm for ongoing trade relationship.
- Positive Maori visits to Australia and England.
- Positive links with Britain, back to Cook's first visits.
- Trusted role of missionaries.
- Concerns about the French returning for utu. (Or is this underlying?)
- Concerns about French treatment of Tahitians.

Underlying

- Maori were impressed with British power?
- Traditional inter-hapu rivalries?

Activity 5, pp. 74–75

Political	Economic
Paragraph 2: lawlessness, plus asserting authority over any New Zealand Company settlements Paragraph 5: pressure from the humanitarian movement Paragraph 6: British concerns of possible intervention in New Zealand by the US and/ or France	Paragraph 3: concerns of investors
Social	**Technological**
Paragraph 4: Britain's belief in its cultural superiority	None?

Activity 6, p. 75

Political	Economic
Paragraph 1: Shared concerns about Pakeha lawlessness Paragraph 3: A longer history of links with Britain, including governors in Australia Paragraph 4: Maori concerns that another country, especially France, might threaten New Zealand's security Paragraph 5: Emphasis in the Treaty on a strong bond between chiefs and the Queen Paragraph 6: Chiefly authority appeared to be guaranteed in the Treaty	Paragraph 2: Maori desire to continue trade and contact with Europeans. Paragraph 7: Traditional rivalries meant hapu did not want to miss out on the potential benefits of a relationship with the British Crown *(or should this be in political? Or social!?)*
Social	**Technological**
None?	None?

Activity 10, pp. 81–85

Feel free to disagree with where the 'line is drawn' between short and long-term consequence given here! Below are a range of consequences which can be directly linked to the Treaty. You may have different ones; if so, discuss them with the rest of the class.

Short-term consequences (up to the mid-1860s)

- After the signing of the Treaty the British Crown believed itself to be the sole governing authority (although power soon shifted from the governor to a settler parliament).
- George Grey, the most influential of all the governors, arrived in 1845 and set about buying up large amounts of land.
- Military conflict occurred in Northland in 1845 as the expected benefits of the Treaty failed to materialise. A truce and then peace was agreed.
- In reality the governors had little real authority as Maori were still dominant in all meaningful ways. Race relations remained relatively peaceful.
- Economically, Maori were dominant in New Zealand up until the late 1850s, especially in the North Island.
- In 1852 Britain granted the growing number of settlers their own parliament; few Maori were eligible to vote.
- By 1858 the settler population of 59,000 passed that of Maori (56,000), and it was growing at a much greater rate; these numbers represented a change in the political balance of power.
- In 1858 Waikato Maori and their supporters formed their own political organisation, the Kingitanga to look after the lands and interests of the people.
- In the early 1860s around 10,000 British soldiers were brought in to impose Crown authority, defeating the Kingitanga forces.

Long-term consequences (from the mid-1860s)

- Post-war, up to four million acres of fertile Maori land were confiscated, leaving many hapu destitute *[in poverty]*.
- Laws, such as the Native Lands Acts, broke communal land ownership and impoverished Maori; by the end of the century Maori rangatiratanga (political authority) had all but disappeared despite efforts to keep it alive.
- Until 1872, several other significant guerrilla wars continued to plague the east (Te Kooti) and west (Titokowaru) coast of the North Island.
- The large number of settlers benefited from this transfer of land from Maori to themselves and by the end of the century their economy was booming.
- By 1900, disease, war and loss of land had decimated the Maori population; alcohol, debt, and efforts by the government to convert Maori to 'brown Pakeha' through education in the Pakeha system had all taken their toll too.

Activity 12, pp. 86–89

A. British expectations behind presenting Maori with the Treaty

A In the long-term. At first British authority was limited and relief on Maori compliance. The settlers got their own parliament in 1852 but it was the wars of the 1860s where the Crown really asserted its authority over Maori.

B Unclear. The text does mention that Crown authority at first extended only over limited areas populated by settlers, but it does say that race relations were relatively peaceful.

C Almost fully met in the long-term (up to 1900). Maori ways and customs were restricted to a few rural and isolated areas where they were 'out of sight, out of mind'.

D Fully met, it would seem, in the long-term. The settler population by 1900 was around 750,000, having surpassed the Maori population from 1858.

E Fully, both in the short-term and long-term.

F Unclear; there is no mention of the French so perhaps this means that they ceased to exist as a possible 'threat'.

B. Main reasons why many Maori signed up to the Treaty

A Unclear. The text does mention that Crown authority at first extended only over limited areas populated by settlers, but it does say that race relations were relatively peaceful.

B In the short-term, up until the early 1860s. The text talks about Maori dominating the local economy and even exporting to Australia and California. Settler populations were at first reliant on Maori for food.

C In the short-term only, up until the early 1860s (although Heke and Kawiti fought with the Crown in 1845 before peace was re-established). Clearly the wars of the 1860s and beyond marked a severe deterioration in relations.

D Unclear. Perhaps the same evidence for 'B' applies here too.

E In the short-term only. It says that in 1852 the settlers got their own parliament: 'The power of the governor (and thus, the British Crown) was greatly restricted; the "covenant", it seemed, had ended.'

F In the short-term only, while the governor's authority only extended to the Pakeha settlements (without Maori compliance). While their rangatiratanga might not have been accepted by the British, it was only after the wars of the 1860s that it was effectively ended. 'By the end of the century, Maori rangatiratanga (political authority) had all but disappeared except for in a few remote areas, ... [despite] vigorous efforts to keep it alive ...'

ISBN: 9780170418393

Activity 1, pp. 91–93

1) **Generalisation**: Politically, after the signing of the Treaty, the British Crown believed itself to be the sole governing authority, although power soon shifted from the governor to a settler parliament.

Possible specific evidence

- William Hobson died in 1842 and was replaced by Robert FitzRoy, who in turn was replaced in 1845 by George Grey.
- [The governors passed] some laws affecting land, kauri felling and customs payments.
- By 1865 just 1% of the South Island remained in Maori ownership.
- Still, initially Pakeha authority did not much affect Maori beyond a few populated areas such as Nelson, Whanganui and Auckland.
- [In] 1852 Britain granted them this right [granted settlers their own parliament].
- By 1858 the settler population of 59,000 passed that of Maori (56,000), and it was growing at a much greater rate; these numbers represented a change in the political balance of power.

2) **Generalisation:** In 1858, Waikato Maori and their supporters formed their own political organisation, the Kingitanga, but this move was seen as a threat by the government.

Possible specific evidence

- [Maori appointed a] king, Potatau Te Wherowhero.
- Such an organisation was quite in line with Maori understanding of Articles 1 and 2 of the Treaty, which established a partnership.
- In the early 1860s around 10,000 British soldiers were brought in to impose Crown authority.
- [The] settler parliament was able to break further resistance through the use of the law, such as the Native Lands Acts, which broke communal land ownership.
- By the end of the century, Maori rangatiratanga (political authority) had all but disappeared except for in a few remote areas, such as Aotea (Great Barrier Island). There were, however, vigorous efforts to keep it alive, including the formation of two Maori parliaments, Kotahitanga and Kauhanganui.

3) **Generalisation**: Although military conflict was not common, wars did occur in Northland in 1845 and, most significantly, in the central North Island in the 1860s.

Possible specific evidence

- Hone Heke ... chopped down the flagstaff at Kororareka (Russell). Despite bringing in over 500 troops from Australia, Governor FitzRoy and then Grey could not defeat Heke and Kawiti, but nor could Heke and Kawiti defeat the British.
- [The] main wars of the 1860s (in Taranaki and the Waikato) resulted in an eventual loss for the numerically inferior Maori forces ... 500 Maori faced 1400 British troops at Rangiriri in November 1863.
- [Several] other significant guerrilla wars continued to plague the east and west coasts of the North Island, involving Te Kooti and Titokowaru respectively.
- By 1872, the last shots of the New Zealand Wars had been fired and Maori military resistance was at an end.

4) **Generalisation**: Economically, Maori were dominant in New Zealand up until the late 1850s, especially in the North Island.

Possible specific evidence

- In a variety of places such as Waikato they had vast fields of crops, which helped to feed the new settlements such as Wellington and New Plymouth.
- The politician William Swainson described extensive farming activity among Te Arawa, Tuwharetoa and Mataatua iwi.
- By the early 1850s ... exports to the Australian and Californian goldfields ...
- Flour mills to grind wheat for bread were common features of the Maori landscape, such as at Whanganui, Rotorua and Wairarapa.
- However, an economic slump in the mid-1850s and then the wars of the 1860s dealt Maori a severe economic blow.
- After the wars of the 1860s, up to four million acres of fertile Maori land were confiscated, leaving many hapu destitute *[in poverty]*.
- Between 1872 and 1900, some eight million acres of land shifted into Pakeha ownership. By 1939, Maori held only about 9% of the land in New Zealand.

Activity 1, pp. 95–98

1 **Possible response**

It would seem that there has not previously been a commemoration of the New Zealand/Land Wars, which suggests that the government has had no interest in remembering this part of our past (unlike WWI/WWII through ANZAC Day). However, some schools at least are teaching their students about the conflict (eg Otorohanga High School) and this has prompted them to action. The 12,000 petition signers suggest that there is a desire to learn more and, although it took six years, the government has agreed to begin commemorations. Thus the wars of the 1860s (past), neglected in our national memory for so long, will finally be publicly recognised each year (present). It will be interesting to see the response of New Zealanders to this commemoration.

2 **Possible response**

The Gallipoli landing was commemorated immediately, becoming a public holiday within five years, so it had importance to people at the time (past). It is still commemorated nationwide today (present) and in fact the numbers attending have increased substantially, especially since the 1980s when there was little interest (according to historian Jock Phillips). This could be considered strange given that the campaign was a 'disaster'. However, being the centenary of the landing the large numbers are probably to be expected, even though it is not just in 2015 that large crowds attended. The chief executive of the RSA says that people want to remember not just WWI but also others who serve in the military. ANZAC Day commemorations stand in contrast to commemorations of the New Zealand Wars, which have taken until 2017 to be officially recognised.

3 **Possible response**

Kristine Bartlett was able to bring a case for equal pay based on the 1972 Equal Pay Act (past), so it is still relevant in the present (or near present) day. However, the fact that she had to shows that, despite the law passed all those years ago, there is still a gender pay gap, at least in the aged care sector. This might tell us that things haven't changed as much from 1972 as women at least might hope. It would be interesting to see if other cases of a gender pay gap are brought to the courts.

4 **Possible response**

Although relations between New Zealand and the US were strained by the refusal to allow entry of the warship in 1985 (past), by 2016 (present) they had improved enough for New Zealand (under a National government) to invite a US warship visit and for the US to accept it. Interestingly, the anti-nuclear law is still in effect but there is no longer strong public reaction to the ship visit, especially compared to 35,000 protesters who turned out when the Truxton came in 1983. It seems, then, that while the anti-nuclear position of New Zealand is important to people (the law hasn't been changed) there is no longer such strong sentiment against US ship visits.

Activity 2, pp. 101–102

1 Possible revised question: 'Do you think that it should be a requirement to vaccinate dogs?' (By using the word 'responsible' in the question, pet owners who don't vaccinate their pets are, by implication, irresponsible.)

2 Possible revised question: 'If you have a favourite band/musical group, what is it?' (It may well be that the respondents don't like punk, so have no favourite punk band. How can they answer the question?)

3 Possible revised question: 'How happy or unhappy are you with the current level of school funding?' And, next possible question: 'What do you think of the NCEA?' (The original question is asking a lot of the respondents. Some might try to answer both questions, but many others will concentrate on the one that means the most to them.)

4 Possible revised question: 'How many nights a week do you usually shower before bed?' (For many people, the answer to the original question will be no, as they shower in the morning.)

Activity 3, pp. 105–106

Your responses may differ slightly from those given here.

Source A

a 38% **b** 7% **c** 34%

Source B

a 24% **b** 30% **c** 36%
d 10%

Source C

a 13% **b** 20% **c** 7%
d 49% **e** 8%

Source D

Slow increase from about 600,000 in 1735 to about one million in 1820, then there is a reasonably steady increase up to just over five million in 2014 – or similar.

Source E

Although a little uneven, there is a steady rise in the catch from 200,000 tonnes in 1950 to 600,000 tonnes in 2000. Thereafter there is a sharper drop to 500,000 tonnes in 2010 before the beginnings (?) of another sharp rise after 2010 – or similar.

Source F

All three sets of data are not linear but patterns can be discerned *[seen]*. One anomaly *[variation]* is a sharp rise in the years 2012–13. The overall annual losses trend appears to be a steady rise from 30% losses in 2011 to 44% by 2016. The winter losses had trended downwards between 2008 and 2012 (then there was the sharp rise as mentioned previously), but, after flattening out 2013–15, appear to be trending steadily upward again to about 28% losses by 2016. Finally, the summer losses share a generally similar pattern to the winter losses, although the loss rate is about 5% lower until matching or exceeding the winter losses in 2014 (at 23%) – or similar.

Activity 1, pp. 119–123

Map 1 possible points to cover

- This map looks at how the various (named) electorates in New Zealand voted in the 2016 existing versus alternative flag referendum. It is worth noting that as a map/graphic it is easier to interpret and see quickly the outcome than just a table of results.
- It shows that in only six electorates (two in Auckland, Bay of Plenty, three in the South Island) there was a majority for change; although there are no figures to back this up, it looks from this resource as though the vote to keep the existing flag was greater. (It was!)
- While there is no key that states this, it might be that the darker the red colour of an electorate the stronger the vote for retaining the existing flag.
- As the source is the Electoral Commission it is likely to be a reliable and factual presentation of the results.
- Presumably the statistics from which this graphic was generated came from the actual number of votes cast. It would be useful to see these figures to compare them with the graphic to confirm its accuracy.

Map 2 possible points to cover

- This map looks at Palestinian land loss between the years of 1946 and 2010; Palestinian land is in green and Jewish land in white. Over the time frame of the map the amount of land of Palestine reduces significantly and becomes more 'patchy' while the amount of Jewish land increases and becomes less 'patchy'. There is no scale, which would be good to have, so it is difficult to tell how big the total land area is. The map is produced in 2012, two years after the last date of the land loss shown, so it is reasonably up-to-date at that time.
- The only other significant feature on the series of maps is the label 'UN Plan' in 1947 – it's not clear what this is so that would need further research. Nor is there any indication why the land area for Palestine is reducing over time.
- The source is *Journal of World Literature Today*, presumably based at the University of Oklahoma. It's unclear what the link is here with literature but as a University-based source it should have at least a degree of reliability. It's not clear where the data came from to produce this map; presumably from land sale/use records? This would need to be checked out.

Map 3 possible points to cover

- This map is of the city of El Paso in Texas, 1886. There is no obvious scale and although there is evidence of writing on the map (eg street names) it is too small to read – a magnifying glass will be needed! There is no map compass but presumably north is at the top of the map.
- The city is mostly flat and has mountains to the north and a river to the south. The central part seems more built up, although there are no really tall buildings – there might be a church/cathedral just to the east of the centre. The streets are set out in a grid pattern. Two bridges cross the river so presumably this city is connected to others by road, river and rail. The trees along the riverbank are so evenly spaced that they may have been planted. There appear to be three (maybe four) railway lines with what looks like a fairly big central railway station, so this city appears to be quite a hub. There seems to be some sort of crops planted in the northeast.
- Augustus Koch is a map-maker, but that's all we know about who created this and why. This would need more research. He's created a 'bird's-eye view' – maybe there are mountains to the south from which he could see the city; if not it would be hard to create such a map from ground-level. Perhaps he used city council records to help out, too (if there were such records kept in 1886). Presumably he was paid to produce this as it's quite a lot of effort to go to; it's not clear who would have commissioned this map – the city council? If so, maybe Koch would want to make the city look more prosperous than it really was.
- It would be good to find out more about Koch and his 'qualifications'. A 'zoomed out' map would also be useful to see where El Paso is located in Texas/the US.

Map 4 possible points to cover

- This map has no title (or scale) but it appears to be looking at migration from Southeast Asia into the Pacific, including New Zealand; presumably this is the Polynesian peoples. The text descriptions alongside the map support this. The timescale runs from 'Before 3000BC' through to the most recent date, the 1200AD arrival at New Zealand (circled on the map). A triangle shape runs from New Zealand in the south to Rapanui/Easter Island in the east to Hawaii in the north. This matches the text 'Colonisation of East Polynesia, and dispersal to remote islands (including Hawaii, Easter Island, and New Zealand).
- The source dates in the text – 2009 and 2011 – suggest that this map was produced some time around then, and the publications mentioned appear to be reputable and unbiased: *Science* and 'Proceedings of the National Academy of Sciences of the USA'.
- There is no explanation of the different coloured arrows; presumably the pink ones are the Polynesians. Other documents and publications would help check the information in this map.

Map 5 possible points to cover

- This map is of the British Empire in 1910, with a title/ explanation on it saying that the flags of the countries shown are part of a 'free empire' showing 'British power throughout the word'. This sounds a lot like propaganda and the fact that the map is produced by the British government supports this. A lot of the flags have the British Union Jack on them.
- Some countries, including New Zealand, Australia and Canada, are coloured pink on the map; other smaller countries might be too but it is too hard to see. There is a lot of small text but it is too hard to read without a magnifying glass.
- The purpose of this map would seem to be to send a message about the extent and power of the British Empire. This might be to warn off any potential enemies as well as instil pride in its 'members'. It would be interesting to see how many people within this Empire don't feel this level of pride; Maori and Aborigines, perhaps.

ISBN: 9780170418393